FACES OF

EXHIBITION
Organized by the Americas Society
Curated by N. C. Christopher Couch

AMERICAS SOCIETY / ART GALLERY
New York, New York
September 19–December 15, 1991

NORTH CAROLINA MUSEUM OF ART
Raleigh, North Carolina
May 19–July 31, 1992

*The Americas Society gratefully acknowledges
the Samuel H. Kress Foundation, the National Endowment
for the Arts, and the New York State Council on the Arts
for their support of this exhibition. The education
program is funded in part by a grant from the Fundación
Angel Ramos.*

FACES OF ETERNITY

MASKS OF THE PRE-COLUMBIAN AMERICAS

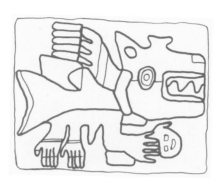

by N. C. Christopher Couch

AMERICAS SOCIETY
New York

AMERICAS SOCIETY

The Americas Society is the only national not-for-profit institution devoted exclusively to educating the United States public about all facets of our Western Hemisphere neighbors. The goal of the Society is to foster an understanding of contemporary political, social and economic issues confronting Latin America, the Caribbean and Canada, and to increase public awareness and appreciation of the rich cultural heritage of our neighbors.

The Society strives to achieve its mission through a variety of programs offered by its three major divisions: Latin American Affairs, Canadian Affairs, and Cultural Affairs.

COVER ILLUSTRATION
Mosaic face mask

Mixtec, Acatlan, Puebla, Mexico

Postclassic, A.D. 1200–1500

wood, paint, stone tesserae

16.5 x 13.7 x 7 cm

National Museum of the American Indian, Smithsonian Institution, New York, New York

[CAT NO. 55]

OFFICERS

David Rockefeller
Chairman

Marifé Hernández
John S. Reed
Vice Chairmen

George W. Landau
President

Ludlow Flower III
Executive Vice President

Susan Kaufman Purcell
Vice President

John E. Avery, Jr.
Secretary

Charles E. Barber
Treasurer

DEPARTMENT OF VISUAL ARTS

Thomas M. Messer
Senior Counselor for the Arts

Fatima Bercht
Director

Barbara Berger
Visual Arts and Education Programs Administrator

Randolph S. Black
Gallery Manager

Julie Van Voorhis
Administrative Assistant

Sandra Antelo-Suarez
John Farmer
Felix Gil
Lisa Leavitt
Rebekah Sidman
Evidalia Saez
Gallery Assistants

Elizabeth Ferrer
Curatorial and Special Projects Consultant

Ana Sokoloff
Curatorial and Special Projects Consultant

DEPARTMENT OF DEVELOPMENT

Elizabeth Beim
Director

Linda Friedman
Assistant to the Director

MEMBERSHIP

Judith Watson
Membership Secretary

EDUCATION

Barbara Berger
Education Coordinator

Catalina Parra
Workshop Coordinator

VISUAL ARTS ADVISORY BOARD

Wilder Green
Chairman

Patricia Cisneros

Barbara D. Duncan

Yolanda Garza Lagüera

Marifé Hernández

George W. Landau

William S. Lieberman

Craig Morris

Waldo Rasmussen

Roger D. Stone

Elizabeth A. Straus

John N. Stringer

Edward J. Sullivan

Catalogue

Copyright 1991 Americas Society

Library of Congress Card Catalogue Number 91–074083

ISBN 1-879128-03-9

Published by the Americas Society
680 Park Avenue
New York, NY 10021

CONTENTS

ACKNOWLEDGMENTS

THIS YEAR, AS THE PEOPLE and nations of the Americas and Europe begin commemoration of the quincentennial of Christopher Columbus's voyage to the New World, the Americas Society will also be marking an anniversary—a quarter of a century of exhibitions, publications and special programs focusing on the culturally diverse artistic traditions of Latin America, the Caribbean and Canada.

To inaugurate a special series of exhibitions and events organized in observance of Columbus's 1492 voyage and our twenty-fifth anniversary, the Americas Society is pleased to present *Faces of Eternity: Masks of the Pre-Columbian Americas*, the first exhibition ever organized to focus exclusively on the mask-making traditions of the native cultures of North, Central and South America and the Caribbean, prior to the Europeans' arrival in the New World.

The realization of *Faces of Eternity: Masks of the Pre-Columbian Americas* has been made possible through the cooperation of many individuals and institutions.

On the behalf of the Americas Society, I offer my sincere thanks to the following individuals in Lima, Peru: Dr. Carlos Torres y Torres Lara, Ministro de Relaciones Exteriores; Dr. Oscar de la Puente Raygada, Ministro de Educación; Ambassador Ricardo V. Luna, Permanent Representative to the United Nations from Peru; and Dr. Roberto Vélez Arce, Director General de Relaciones Culturales Internacionales, Ministerio de Relaciones Exteriores. I would also like to thank Dr. Pedro Gjurinovic Canevaro, Jefe del Instituto Nacional de Cultura; the insititute is responsible for allowing loans of artwork from the museums under its administration. My special thanks go to Ambassador Anthony C. E. Quainton, at the U.S. Embassy in Lima.

The Americas Society is grateful to Allen Wardwell, who initiated this project several years ago and contributed his invaluable knowledge on the subject of native cultures to its supervision. We must also offer special thanks to the curator of the exhibition, Dr. Christopher Couch, Assistant Professor of Pre-Columbian Art, Smith College, Northampton, Massachusetts, for his enthusiasm and dedication to *Faces of Eternity*, which is an insightful, important contribution to the field.

I would like to extend my deepest appreciation to the museums and art collectors in Ecuador, Peru and the United States, who have so kindly allowed their artworks to be shown in this exhibition.

The Americas Society wishes to acknowledge the generous support received from the Fundación Angel Ramos, Samuel H. Kress Foundation, National Endowment for the Arts, and the New York State Council on the Arts.

We are also indebted to the members of the Visual Arts Advisory Board for their much appreciated guidance and support.

George W. Landau
PRESIDENT

FOREWORD

THE DEPARTMENT OF VISUAL ARTS of the Americas Society is very pleased to present *Faces of Eternity: Masks of the Pre-Columbian Americas*. This exhibition and its accompanying catalogue study mask-making traditions of over thirty-five cultures active in the Americas during the preconquest period. The unique grouping of these Pre-Columbian masks and mask-wearing figures reminds us of the complexity and diversity of social, religious and artistic values held by Native Americans, in many instances centuries before the voyages of exploration that brought the European colonizers to American shores. Although our information on the cultural contexts in which the masks were created is often fragmentary, we are able to observe the skill with which the masks' creators portrayed themselves, their gods, and other mythological beings. These masks speak clearly to us, across the centuries, of the aspirations of their makers.

The idea for a series of exhibitions celebrating the extremely rich traditions of mask-making in the Americas was first presented several years ago by Allen Wardwell to John Stringer, then director of the Americas Society Visual Arts Department. It is a great satisfaction to present *Faces of Eternity*, the first, I hope, in a series of exhibitions that will examine the continuing tradition of masking in the Americas.

I would like to thank Allen Wardwell for his initial, enlightened idea, and the support he offered to us and Dr. Christopher Couch, curator of *Faces of Eternity*, throughout this project. We are thankful we had the opportunity to collaborate with Dr. Couch, whose dedicated curatorship and scholarly insights have made this exhibition, and its accompanying catalogue, a significant contribution to our better understanding the Pre-Columbian cultures of the Americas.

On behalf of the Americas Society, I would like to join Dr. Couch in thanking the many museum professionals and scholars who assisted in the preparation of this complex project. *Bogotá, Colombia*: Dr. Clemencia Plazas, at the Museo del Oro, Banco de la República; and Dr. Marianne Cardale Shrimpff. *Guayaquil, Ecuador*: Dr. Olaf Holm, Director, Museo Antropológico, Banco Central de Ecuador. *Lambayeque, Peru*: Dr. Walter Alva, Director, Museo Arqueológico Regional Bruning. *Lima, Peru*: Pedro Gjurinovic Canevaro, Jefe del Instituto Nacional de Cultura; Sra. Rosa Amano, Directora, Museo Amano; Fernando de Szyszlo; Francisco Fariña Tweddle; Dr. Arturo Jimenez Borja, Director, Museo de la Nación; Sra. Isabel Larco de Alvarez-Calderón, Directora, Museo Arqueológico Rafael Larco Herrera; Maria Angélica Matarazzo de Benavides; Hilda Paloma and Miguel Cordoba, Ministerio de Relaciones Exteriores, Departamento de Asuntos Culturales. At the Museo Nacional de Arqueología y Antropología: Dr. Herminio Rosas La Noire, Director; Sra. Beatriz Benavides Prado, Directora de Relaciones Públicas; and Dr. Peter Kvietok, Director Museografía. Dra. Guadalupe Salas, Directora General de Museos, Instituto Nacional de Cultura; Dr. Francisco Statsny; and Dr. Guillermo Wiese de Osma.

In the *United States*, advice and assistance were lent by: Dr. Warren Barbour, State University of New York, Buffalo / Joan Barist / At the Brooklyn Museum, Department of African, Oceanic, and New World Art: Sue Bergh, Assistant Curator; Diana Fane, Curator; and Lois Martin, Research Associate / At the National Museum of the American Indian, Smithsonian Institution: Lee Callandar, Registrar; Mary Purdy, Assistant Registrar; Nancy Rosoff, Curator, Middle and South American Ethnology; and Adams Taylor, former Collections Manager / Cynthia Conides, Columbia University / At the American Museum of Natural History, Department of Anthropology: Barbara Conklin, Registrar; Belinda Kaye, Registrar for Loans and Archives; Dr. Craig Morris, Curator; Vuka Roussakis, Textile Conservator; and William Weinstein, Systems Analyst / Dr. Thomas B. F. Cummins, Department of Art History, Virginia Commonwealth University / Sonna Deutsch, Registrar, Honolulu Academy of Arts / Dr. Virginia Fields, Associate Curator of Pre-Columbian Art, Los Angeles County Museum of Art / Dr. Michael Gramley, Curator of Archaeology, Buffalo Museum of Science / Gloria Greis, Archaeological Collections Manager, Peabody Museum of Archaeology and Ethnology, Harvard University / Dr. Maarten van de Guchte, Curator, Krannert Art Museum / Dr. Armand Labbé, Chief Curator, Bowers Museum / At the Merrin Gallery: Edward Merrin, Director; and Linda Schildkraut, Associate Director / Dr. Esther Pasztory, Department of Art History and Archaeology, Columbia University / Dr. Barbara Purdy, Department of Anthropology, University of Florida, Gainesville / Anne-Louise Schaffer, Curator, Art of the Americas, Africa, and Oceania, the Museum of Fine Arts, Houston / Dr. Carolyn Tate, Associate Curator of Pre-Columbian Art, Dallas Museum of Art / Nora E. Wagner, Curator of Education, the Mexican Museum / At the Hudson Museum, University of Maine, Orono: Dr. Steven Whittington, Director; and Gretchen Faulkner, Development Director / Lucy Williams, Keeper of the American Collection, University Museum, University of Pennsylvania / Margaret Young-Sanchez, Assistant Curator for Later Western Art, Cleveland Museum of Art.

My sincere thanks also to Sonia Labarthe, in charge of cultural affairs at the Consulate of Peru, New York, and Maria Cecilia Rozas Britto, Cultural Attaché, at the Embassy of Peru in Washington, D.C. At the Americas Society, special thanks must be given to Ludlow Flower III, Judith Watson, and Elizabeth Beim for their help. Barbara Berger, Visual Arts Programs Administrator, and Randolph Black, Gallery Manager, should be commended for their tireless devotion to the project, as should Gwen Allen, for her research and editorial work on the catalogue and exhibition labels. The assistance of Felix Gil, Lisa Leavitt, and Julie Van Voorhis is also much appreciated, as are the conservation skills of Ellen Pearlstein. The good work of a talented team of editors including Joanna Eckman, Jacquelyn Hamm Southern, and Daniel Jussim should also be recognized.

Fatima Bercht
DIRECTOR
DEPARTMENT OF VISUAL ARTS

PREFACE

M ASKS OF VARIOUS KINDS are included in almost every survey of Pre-
Columbian art. They might be life-size or even larger, or miniatures, representing replicas of types that were worn by shamans, ceremonial
performers, rulers, or warriors. They might be of stone, ceramic, or such
metals as copper, gold, or silver; there are even a small number of perishable wood or cloth. Furthermore, some of the imagery that appears on
Pre-Columbian frescoes, vase paintings, relief carvings and sculptures
shows people wearing or carrying masks.

It is evident that masks were an important ceremonial component in
the ancient Americas, and yet, to our knowledge, this is the first exhibition to focus on the subject of their use and style. The reasons for this
oversight are difficult to surmise. As this exhibition and publication
prove, masks are every bit as interesting, arresting, and beautiful as the
better-known figure sculptures, paintings, and relief carvings. They also
provide intriguing glimpses into the customs, beliefs, and ceremonial life
of earlier times.

The Random House Dictionary defines a mask as "a covering for all or
part of the face, usually worn to conceal identity." In the context of any
indigenous society that employs masks as a part of its ritual observances,
such a description is woefully inadequate. We are reminded of Roger Caillois's observation that "peoples gain access to history and civilization the
moment they reject the mask, when they repudiate it as a medium of collective panic, and when it is bereft of its central and institutional function.... Its creation is no longer associated with magic, but with art."
(Hainaux 1961)

Although Caillois's "collective panic" may be something of an overstatement, the magical function to which he refers was all-important in ancient and largely preliterate cultures. It gave to the mask a significance that is impossible for us to fully comprehend. Because the use of the mask is so widespread throughout many different indigenous societies of the world from early times, it must satisfy a basic human need. It is probable that masks were first worn by shamans to help them communicate with the supernatural realm. It is also likely that, because shamanism is humanity's oldest system of beliefs, masks were among the earliest ritual objects made. They were worn to reenact shamanic journeys, to tell stories relating to the acquisition of power, and to identify the nature of the shaman's spirit helper. The actual donning of a mask enabled the shaman to take on the magical properties and characteristics of the being represented and sometimes even to become the temporary locus of the spirit itself. Masks of this kind were objects that inspired feelings of awe and fear in anyone who encountered them.

These are the transformation masks that fall into Christopher Couch's first category in this catalogue. As he suggests, the motivation for the creation of the other mask types of ancient America stemmed from the same need to give tangible form to supernatural and spiritual powers. Whether they were used for burial, in ceremonial performances, as architectural decoration, or even as representations of individuals as part of the paraphernalia of the state, masks called to mind some aspect of this other world. They could be realistic or idealized portraits, grotesque or inventive combinations of human and animal features, forms abstracted to a point of minimalism, or highly ornate creations including representations of such extraneous material as textiles, feathers, jewelry, or animal and bird heads. In other words, the masks follow the same stylistic and iconographic formulas to be found in more familiar art forms.

Despite these congruences, however, the fact remains that many of the surviving masks of Pre-Columbian America such as those shown in this publication are in a sense incomplete. Once removed from their original settings, all masks are only a part of what they once were. If they were used for burial, they have been taken from the grave, the body, and the offerings with which they were originally associated, and in only a few cases do we know whose body it was. If they were shamanic, their symbolism is now lost. If they were used in state displays or public festivals, the accompanying costumes and ritual paraphernalia (mentioned by Dr. Couch as being at least as important as the masks themselves) have long since been lost. Some of the masks here provide tantalizing glimpses of resplendent ceremonies that will never be known to us. If they were architectural ornaments, they are no longer seen in the context of their now unknown structures.

Most of the masks used for ritual purposes throughout the world are made of such ephemeral materials as wood, animal hide, textiles, plant fibers, and feathers. This was the case in Pre-Columbian Mexico and Guatemala, as can be seen from depictions in many of the relief carvings, sculptures, and paintings from this period. Great traditions of mask-making once existed from which little or nothing has survived. To give just one example, some of the scenes in the Maya murals of Bonampak represent a panoply of fantastic masked performers of animal and semihuman creatures. Their face coverings must have been among the most extraordinary inventions of the mask-maker's art ever created, and yet nothing of the originals remains today.

Nevertheless, it is fortunate that so much evidence of this rich tradition has survived in two-dimensional and sculptural re-creations as well as in the many masks and maskettes from which the examples of this exhibition were chosen. These small pieces of stone, ceramic, metal, and cloth are works of art yielding insights into aspects of ceremonial and social life in ancient America that we have just begun to study.

Allen Wardwell

INTRODUCTION

In the pre-columbian americas, masks were made and used from the earliest times to the conquest. They were ubiquitous in both hemispheres, among cultures of all types—from hunter-gatherers to agricultural communities to imperial states. Masking was universal and central to public and religious life from the earliest periods until the conquest. Masks were never marginalized in contexts we would identify as theatrical. Rather, they remained fundamental to the language of power, spirituality, and social identity.

Over centuries of tradition and development, the art of masks became greatly refined. Artists worked in media as diverse as feathers, adobe, textiles, ceramics, stone, metal, and gems. They adapted masks to rites, where they formed an element of costume; burials, where they were ritually interred with the dead; and even architecture, where they became monumental elements of buildings and related sculptures. The art of mask-making remained profoundly expressive of societies throughout the Americas until the conquest.

Pre-Columbian masks fall into a number of categories. Face masks, with or without eyes and mouths pierced through, are the size and approximate shape of the human face. Helmet masks cover the entire head, and may even extend down the torso; these were made of perishable materials, probably wooden frames covered with cloth, skin, or feathers, and are known through models and images. Miniature masks are smaller than the human face, and while most were worn like jewelry, some were used to cover part of the face. Mouth masks, especially characteristic of the Peruvian South Coast, are relatively large objects made of sheet gold which covered the lower half of the face, except the mouth. Monumental masks and masked sculptures formed part of the architectural ensemble of public and ritual spaces.

Masking appears to have been more important in Mesoamerica than in other regions of Pre-Columbian America. To some extent, however, this must be attributed to the loss of the majority of masks, which were surely made of perishable materials. No masks are preserved from the southwestern United States, although petroglyphs and images on Mimbres ceramics preserve records of their use. Exceptional cases—like the preservation of Late Mississippian masks in the swamps of Florida, rare finds in caves and tombs in Mesoamerica, and grave goods from the desert coast of Peru which include both masks and textiles showing masking—allow a glimpse of what has been lost.

Miniature mask
Tlatilco, Mexico
Preclassic, 1150–550 B.C.
11.5 cm
The Brooklyn Museum, Brooklyn, New York, 59.237.4
[NOT EXHIBITED]

The tremendous variety of Pre-Columbian masks is inseparable, both formally and iconographically, from larger social and cultural systems, including traditions of masking, song, dance, and myth. Within societies, there are significant icons in which the innovations and subtle interpretations of individual artists may be understood. Further, masks are part of the symbolic system of a culture, and the striking formal and symbolic oppositions between them reflect transformations within a single system (Levi-Strauss 1982). For example, such an opposition appears in the pairing of Tlaloc—the rain god of the agricultural civilizations of Mesoamerica, with his round, protruding eye ornaments and mouth with projecting fangs—and Xipe Totec, a god of warfare and human sacrifice, whose flayed skin mask opens at the eyes and mouth to reveal the human face beneath (cat. no. 59, illustrated) (cat no. 70). Between cultures, one canon may be adopted and adapted. For example, the Aztecs made turquoise mosaic masks of the merchant god; a Mayan example is known in silver; and there is a Huastec work in ceramic with face-painting (cat. no. 46, illustrated) (Klein 1986, 138–39).

In addition, each mask may be considered mutable under varying conditions. Its appearance may change according to whether it is seen during the day or night, inside a building, or outside in a plaza or temple precinct. Motion in dance and ritual also affects masks: "Shapes, textures, colors, and patterns . . . move within a kaleidoscope of balances and oppositions of motion and speed" (Cole 1985, 17). Finally, the same mask may appear to be quite different to different audiences. Fray Diego Durán describes the festival of Xipe Totec, in the ceremonial period called Tlacaxipehualizti, when the rulers of tributary states were brought to the Templo Mayor to witness sacrifices of the conquered. The Tlaloc masks of the priests who performed the sacrifices would have had very different meanings for the hosts and guests, respectively (Durán 1967, II:228).

Wearing a mask can create a sudden and total change in identity. The wearer is transformed, or he disappears to be replaced by another being. Masking thus creates a paradox: the normal social identity of the wearer can no longer be determined from his appearance (Napier 1986, 16).

Masks, and the transformations they render perceptible, make mediation between the human and supernatural realms possible. By wearing a mask, a ritual actor contacts the supernatural through transformation and mimesis. A mask may transform the wearer—shaman, priest, or ruler—into a supernatural being. A masquerade may incarnate deities or ancestors, bringing them into the community to receive offerings, petitions, and thanks.

Masks and the wearing of masks are most often associated with a change in status or condition, especially during the important crises of human life and human society. In many societies, masks play important roles in ceremonies that mark transitions such as the passage to adulthood and times of physical or supernatural danger to the individual or the community. The paradox of masking—the immediate and complete change of identity—parallels changes in status and identity that occur in moments of personal or social crisis: "the transforming role of masks is developmentally most dramatic in their association with the greatest paradox of all—that is, with creation and destruction, birth and death" (Napier 1986, 18).

Funerary masks were important in Pre-Columbian America, and now represent the majority of archaeologically known masks. Some were apparently portraits of the deceased (for example, jade mosaic masks placed over the faces of rulers in Mayan tombs, like that of King Pacal at Palenque). In Central America, the faces of the dead were covered with clay and gold in a type of death mask; these masks are also portraits of the dead (Stone 1972, 12).

Other funerary masks may create a different identity for the dead, idealizing or transforming the person. The mummy bundle of the Aztec emperor was dressed in the masks of four gods who symbolized the qualities of rulership and the historical legitimacy of the throne (Klein 1986). Masks also may indicate actual transformation into a deity; the elite burials of Moche, on the north coast of Peru, often feature masks representing a cross-fanged god (cat. nos. 16, 28, illustrated). Bridging the categories of portraiture and transformation are a variety of stylized or idealized masks such as the Colima burial masks which closely resemble the faces of ceramic sculptures (cat. no. 3), or the idealized faces of Olmec burials which subtly combine deity features or iconography with sensitively modeled human faces (cat. no. 48, illustrated) (Pernet 1987; Brunius 1987).

Because a large number of masks have perished with time, and because of the extraordinary fragility of some that have survived, no exhibition could come close to presenting a complete picture of masks in Pre-Columbian America. In addition, it is difficult to reconstruct the context of archaeological works. Even when the excavation is controlled and fully recorded, most of the culture that produced the object has vanished. Some of the function or use of a mask can be inferred from its form. If eyes and mouth are not pierced through, it probably was funerary; if made of rare or imported materials, it belonged to a member of the elite. However, it is no longer possible to discover and adhere to the original aesthetic and functional categories of artists in preconquest cultures (see Price 1990).

It has rather been our goal to bring together pieces from all of the Americas which, for the most part, are unpublished or rarely seen. We have grouped these masks by broad themes that demonstrate the varied use of masks in the preconquest cultures of the Americas, and that suggest some of their cultural context through analogy, juxtapositions, and oppositions.

These themes are divided broadly into functions—transformation, portraiture, and substitution—and context—state-level societies, architecture, and ritual performance. Naturally, these categories overlap: all masks can be transformational; state-level societies cannot function without public architecture. However, the identification of purpose and symbolic universe is a means of restoring some of the context to these works.

The exhibition is not limited to the countries of present-day Latin America, but includes masks from the Pre-Columbian period in the United States. Although the interrelationships are not well understood, there were state-level societies in the southwestern and eastern United States that traded with Mesoamerica and shared certain cultural complexes, such as the ball game. In great cities like Tenochtitlan, Mexico; Guachimonton, Jalisco; Moche, Peru; and Cahokia, Illinois, masks were part of the language of power by which the ruling elites legitimized their control of these complex societies.

Thus, although Mesoamerica—Mexico and upper Central America—is usually considered a discrete culture area, the modern borders of the United States and Mexico are not a useful boundary of Pre-Columbian masking traditions. The archaeological record, which mainly preserves the masks of the elite, shows striking similarities in their use by rulers in Mesoamerica and the United States. Throughout the Americas, large city-states constructed ceremonial centers and vast public spaces where masks were incorporated in political and religious rituals. Both employed the transformational imagery of animals and deities, combined with costumes and elaborate paraphernalia. Finally, masks are found in elite burials in Mesoamerica, Central and South America, and North America. In both life and death, masks legitimized the religious and political elites of the Americas.

TRANSFORMATION

Throughout the Pre-Columbian history of the Americas, masks often represented the transformation of human beings into animals and supernaturals. Animals and supernaturals are not, of course, mutually exclusive categories, and the transformational masks of the Pre-Columbian Americas exhibit a range from the purely animal, to combinations of zoomorphic and avian features, to deities whose identifying characteristics seem to have no parallel in human or animal physiognomy (such as the rings surrounding the eyes of Tlaloc).

The animals depicted in these masks are powerful, usually the largest and fiercest found in the environment, whether on the Northwest Coast of North America or the Andean highlands. They are often predators such as the jaguar, symbol of divine kingship for the Aztecs and Maya; the eagle and puma, paired as symbols of the Toltec and Aztec military orders; or the rattlesnake, often associated with lightening and rain.

The most striking examples of transformation are seen in helmet masks, almost always animal in form. These covered the entire head of the wearer, whose face was often visible through the animal's mouth. They were commonly worn with avian or zoomorphic costumes that covered the wearer's entire body, completing the transformation.

Helmet masks and full body-covering animal costumes are depicted in sculptures and on textiles from Mesoamerica and South America, from the Aztec, Mayan, West Mexican, Jama Coaque, Paracas, and other cultures. The costumes that accompanied Aztec masks are known from pictorial manuscripts, and from life-size statues such as that of the eagle warrior discovered in the 1978-80 excavations of the Templo Mayor. Helmet masks appear in two contexts in Aztec society: as the costume of warriors, and as that of the emperor in his role as military ruler (Broda 1970).

The context of helmet masks from West Mexico (the modern states of Colima, Jalisco, and Nayarit) is more difficult to determine. The originals no longer exist, and were surely made in perishable materials. Rather, the helmet masks are depicted in tomb sculptures, where they are shown alone or as parts of costumes. They represent a variety of animals, including killer whales, parrots, crabs, and ducks (cat. no. 1, illustrated). These same animals are also commonly represented by full-figure ceramics found in West Mexican tombs.

The only major animals found in tomb sculptures, but not in the known corpus of helmet masks are the deer and the dog which seem to have had important supernatural attributes. These are the only animals in West Mexican art that are sometimes shown in combined form (dogs with deer antlers). Among the Huicholes who live in Nayarit today, the deer symbolizes the hallucinogenic peyote cactus. Peyote may also have been important to Pre-Columbian West Mexican cultures, given the depictions of peyote in the ceramic sculptures (Furst 1965).

Although these helmet masks are reminiscent of those used by soldiers of Tula and the Aztec empire, West Mexico developed independently of central Mexico. Closer parallels may be found elsewhere.

On the Northwest Coast of North America, helmet masks and zoomorphic costumes were and are used by the Tlingit, Haida, Tsimshian, and Kwakiutl. They are only one among many complex uses of animal imagery in a variety of architectural and social contexts. They depict ancestors, animal spirits, and other supernaturals whose exploits are told and retold in myth, song, and ritual performances. Masks, myths, and dances are collectively owned by lineage groups. The masks employed in public dances establish the ranking of the lineages within the community and confirm the power of the leaders. A similar context may underlie the helmet masks of West Mexico. These emblems also could represent lineages or other corporate or kinship groups. The numerous animals depicted on ceramics might have been lineage symbols, with a use similar to their appearance on feast dishes, spoons, boxes, drums, and other items of prestige and display found in the houses and courtyards of the Northwest Coast.

The helmet masks of West Mexico, Paracas, and Ecuador probably also functioned much like those of the historical Northwest Coast. The use of masks and costumes in ritual performances would have reinforced the hierarchical positions of corporate and kinship groups within these societies. The imagery found in masks for public performances was replicated in a wide variety of prestige goods. Transformation into animals and

Standing figure in avian (parrot) costume
Jama Coaque, Ecuador
Regional Developmental, 500 B.C.–A.D. 500
ceramic
17.5 x 10.5 cm
Museo Antropológico, Banco Central de Ecuador, Guayaquil, Ecuador
[CAT. NO. 13]

supernaturals confirmed the personal power of the heads of lineages, and of the leaders or chiefs of communities (Couch, in press). A similar use of transformational masks is known to have established the power of rulers in kingdoms and states, as among the Aztec.

Richly detailed depictions of similar zoomorphic masks and costumes are found on polychromatic, embroidered textiles from the Paracas Peninsula on the South Coast of Peru (Paul, 1990). The Paracas textiles found in burials were apparently never worn, but were made only to be buried, wrapped around the body to form bundles sometimes more than one and one-half meters in diameter.

These textiles were decorated with multiple woven or embroidered images. The earliest are dominated by depictions of a deity known as the "Oculate Being," shown with large eyes and serpentine forms emerging from its head and body. In later textiles, the Oculate Being takes on animal attributes, and what may be human performers dressed in animal costumes appear. These performers wear bird costumes, with wings and tails hanging behind; killer whale and shark costumes, which cover the head and shoulders while human legs and arms emerge below; and feline masks or headdresses (see illustration, p. 13) (Dwyer 1973; 1975).

Also depicted on the Paracas textiles are figures known as flying shamans, which exhibit the skeletalization sometimes characteristic of shamans, who experience death and rebirth. These figures fall or fly in postures that recall the supernatural flight of shamans to the underworld and the upperworld (Paul and Turpin 1986). Sometimes these shamans are shown wearing masks. Unlike the Mesoamerican helmet masks, those shown on these small embroidered figures do not always reveal the human face. The imagery on these textiles may show the transformation of a human being into a supernatural after death.

Despite the dry climate of the desert, which has preserved the textiles, there are no extant helmet masks or body-covering costumes. However, feather capes have been found which could have been part of a birdman costume. Other costume elements that could have been part of transformational ensembles, such as gold feline mouth masks and ornaments with appendages, are known from the Paracas and later Nazca cultures (Ann Peters, personal communication, 1991) (cat. nos. 9, 10, illustrated).

Although the use of masks in Ecuador may have begun with shell masks, sometimes painted red, from the Valdivia culture (3000-1500 B.C.), masking appears to have been most developed in the Tolita and Jama Coaque cultures of the coast (500 B.C.-A.D. 500) (Burgos 1981). Many ceramic masks—both zoomorphic and human—have been found, but most are miniatures, probably not meant to be worn over the face (Meggers 1966).

The best evidence for masking is seen in the Jama Coaque ceramic figure sculptures which show elaborate costumes of feathers, textiles, and metal ornaments, and masks resembling the helmet masks of Mesoamerica. Some figures wear masks or faces in headdresses, which appear above the human face of the religious actor in the costume. Others are in complete zoomorphic or avian costumes, with helmet masks entirely covering the wearer's head (cat. no. 12) (cat. no. 13, illustrated).

Pre-Columbian masks made to cover only the human face are archaeologically known primarily from burials. Although some must have been made exclusively for burial, the many examples with the eyes and mouth pierced through suggest that these masks were worn by the living as well.

Masks from the Preclassic sites of Central Mexico, often called by the name of the well-known site of Tlatilco, are among the best representations of early Mesoamerican masks (see illustration on p. 14). These masks were worn only over the lower half of the face (that is, over the mouth): the source of human speech and song. Tlatilco-style masks are found in tombs as offerings, not placed over the faces of the dead.

Preclassic Central Mexican sites have yielded ceramic masks and masked figurines in the Olmec style. The local elites of the Central Mexican agricultural communities adopted the iconography of the premier civilization of Preclassic Mesoamerica to enhance their own prestige. In a striking figurine from Tlapacoya, the mask covering the lower half of the figure's face resembles an Olmec face (cat. no. 17). The figurine wears an elaborate costume that is usually identified as the garb and protective gear of a player of the Mesoamerican rubber ball game. Olmec-style figurines and vessels are commonly found in Central Mexican burials, but ceramic masks are quite rare; only two or three are known (cat. no. 15).

The only face masks that have been preserved from West Mexico are human face masks from tombs in Colima and Jalisco (cat. no. 3) (cat. no. 4, illustrated), which follow the conventions of ceramic sculptures in these areas (Winning 1974). Some of the masks are pierced through the eyes and mouth, but most are not. All have suspension holes, suggesting that they were worn by either a corpse or a living performer.

Colima-style face masks are of two types. The most common is rectangular, with sharp features that closely resemble the conventionalized faces of ceramic sculptures (cat. no. 3). The second rarer type has a rounded shape, and softer, more organic features (cat. no. 4, illustrated). Clear depictions of face masks, as distinct from helmet masks, are rare in West Mexican figurative sculpture.

The second type of Colima face mask is depicted in ceramic sculptures, worn both by human beings and by dogs (cat. nos. 5 and 6, illustrated).

Nose and mouth ornament
Late Paracas–Early Nazca, South Coast of Peru
Early Horizon–Early Intermediate, 400 B.C.–A.D. 200
gold
13.9 x 19 cm
The Cleveland Museum of Art, Cleveland, Ohio
[CAT. NO. 9]

Plaque of Oculate Being with appendages
Early Nazca, South Coast of Peru
Early Intermediate, 200 B.C.–A.D. 400
gold
18.4 x 21.5 cm
The Cleveland Museum of Art, Cleveland, Ohio
[CAT. NO. 10]

Figure wearing jaguar helmet mask, probably an incensario
Classic Veracruz, Veracruz, Mexico
Classic, A.D. 600–900
gray ceramic, black asphalt paint, incensario bowl broken from rear of head
36.8 x 22.8 cm
Hudson Museum, University of Maine, Orono, Maine
[CAT. NO.7]

Burials of dogs have been discovered in tombs in the Chalchihuites area of West Mexico. Similar interments have been found as far north as Arizona, and dog bones have been identified in Mayan tombs. The dogs who wear human masks may be the guides of the soul, and the human figures could be impersonators of the deceased after death (Phil C. Weigand, personal communication, 1991).

Dogs are the only animals shown wearing human face masks in West Mexican sculpture. Face masks depicting human features appear to have played an important role in the journey of the soul after death in the cultures of West Mexico. In Mesoamerica, dogs were psychopomps, companions of the dead (Peterson 1990, 66). The Aztecs called the canine deity who played this role Xolotl, and considered him the brother of Quetzalcoatl, the feathered serpent.

Monumental public art from the Preclassic period in Mesoamerica shows rulers, priests, and other elite persons dressed in elaborate costumes, and in a few instances, wearing masks. The most striking example is from the cliff murals at Oxtotitlán, Guerrero, where an individual is shown seated on a platform-shaped throne, wearing an avian helmet mask, probably of an owl (Grove 1970). The heartland of the Olmec civilization was on the Gulf Coast of Mexico, in the modern states of Veracruz and Tabasco, and many of the finest stone masks and miniature masks come from this region (cat. nos. 14, 47, 56) (cat nos. 19, 48, illustrated). They depict idealized human faces, or combine deity features with human ones. Helmet masks and deity face masks appear to have transformed

Olmec rulers into were-jaguar, saurian, and avian supernaturals. These rulers must have served as intermediaries between the human and super-natural worlds. Transformational imagery was used in public and funerary art to declare the legitimacy of the rulers of the Olmec, and of other elites in Mesoamerica who borrowed their iconography.

Standing figure wearing helmet mask of killer whale
West Mexico, Colima, Mexico
Preclassic–Classic, 200 B.C.–A.D. 400
solid ceramic
5 x 7.5 x 5 cm
National Museum of the American Indian, Smithsonian Institution, New York, New York
[CAT. NO. 1]

Dog with human face mask
West Mexico, Colima, Mexico
Preclassic–Classic, 200 B.C.–A.D. 400
burnished red ceramic
22.8 x 38.1 cm
Honolulu Academy of Arts, Honolulu,
Hawaii
[CAT. NO. 5]

◆

Face mask
West Mexico, Colima, Mexico
Preclassic–Classic, 200 B.C.–A.D. 400
burnished red ceramic
20.5 x 18.5 x 7 cm
Bowers Museum, Santa Ana, California
[CAT. NO. 4]

*Standing figure wearing
face mask*
West Mexico, Colima, Mexico
Preclassic–Classic, 200
B.C.–A.D. 400
red ceramic
26 x 11.5 x 16 cm
Private Collection, Cleveland
[CAT. NO. 6]

"Ai Aipec" mask
Moche, North Coast, Peru
Early Intermediate, 200 B.C.–A.D. 600
17 x 23.2 cm
copper with shell inlay
Museo Arqueológico Rafael Larco
Herrera, Lima, Peru
[CAT. NO. 16]

Face mask
Olmec, Central Mexico
Preclassic, 1150–900 B.C.
grayware ceramic
17.7 x 15.8 cm
Krannert Art Museum and Kinkead
Pavilion, University of Illinois at
Champaign-Urbana, Illinois
[CAT. NO. 15]

PORTRAITURE

In the arts of Pre-Columbian America, portraiture in the sense of a realist likeness did not have a prominent place. Thus, in Peru, a tradition of oil portraits of the Inca emperors developed during the colonial period, but there is no evidence for it before the conquest (Cummins, in press).

However, indigenous traditions of portraiture are attested in both the extant arts and Spanish Colonial records. Individuals were identified principally by costume, ornament, face-painting, glyphs, and the depiction of stages in human life, such as death or old age. In preconquest arts, masks played a central role in establishing individual identity and confirming social identity.

For the most part, masks that function as portraits follow the stylistic conventions of the cultures in which they originate. Thus, they adhere to the same aesthetic systems as sculpture, painting, and textiles, and portraits in masks may be categorized similarly. Hence a further paradox of masks: while they may transform an individual, they may also identify him or her as a member of a community or kinship group, or even as a specific person.

Apart from the few named examples, Pre-Columbian portraits cannot now be identified. However, Borgatti (1990) has defined modes of portraiture in African art that provide a basis for discussion of Pre-Columbian art. Her categories include generalized anthropomorphic portraits, representational portraits, and emblematic portraits. Generalized anthropomorphic portraits embody ideals of physical beauty; individuals may be identified through personal decoration or insignia, by biographical allusions, or by content alone (ibid., 43). Representational portraits replicate the physiognomy of the individual; they "originate in a face-to-face relationship between subject and artist" (ibid., 59). Finally, emblematic portraits depend on symbolic associations, consisting of an assemblage of objects such as those placed in graves (ibid., 73).

Examples of generalized anthropomorphic portraits are found in Mixtec and Aztec art, notably in pictorial manuscripts. In these traditions, rulers are idealized in canonical portraits. In Mixtec genealogical and historical manuscripts, individuals are identified by a calendrical name (their date of birth) and surname, indicated by a hieroglyph, costume, mask, or a combination of these (Caso 1977–79).

In Aztec manuscripts, portraits are identified solely by glyphs, as the costumes of rulers almost always consist of the same *tenixyo* (eyes-on-the-border) mantle and turquoise mosaic crown. In rare cases, Aztec rulers wear costumes relevant to particular social or military roles, as in the Codex Vaticanus A, when Mocteuczoma Xocoyotl is depicted as the god Xipe Totec to show his role as a military leader (Corona Nuñez 1964, vol. I). Similarly, when they felt their reign approaching its close, the Aztec emperors had portraits of themselves—identified by glyphs—carved on the rock at Chapultepec, their pleasure garden. Fragments of the carving of Mocteuczoma Xocoyotl, the last emperor, remain, although no other identifiable portraits can be located (Umberger 1981).

By contrast, Mayan portraits are more representational, as are those of some Peruvian cultures. Among the Maya, faces are idealized, but anatomical peculiarities are detailed. For example, at Palenque, members of the ruling dynasty are depicted in stone reliefs and stucco sculptures on the palace and temples. Lady Zac-Kuk, King Pacal's mother, is shown with swollen and clubbed fingers; King Pacal, with a clubfoot; and his son, Chan-Bahlum, with six toes and fingers. The idealization of faces includes the wearing of a prosthetic device over the nose to achieve the perfect Mayan profile (Robertson 1983).

Finally, emblematic portraits may be found in Peruvian and Central American traditions. For example, the rich tomb of the Moche "Old Lord of Sipán," discovered in Peru in 1989, includes paraphernalia of his earthly power and authority, such as masks, ornaments in precious metals and stones, and textile banners with applied metal figures (Alva 1990).

Generalized anthropomorphic portraits

This sort of mask is typical of Mesoamerica. Face-painting was the basic portrait device, interpreted in a variety of media.

Numerous examples of face-painting or tattoos date from Preclassic Mexico. Some Olmec jade masks from Veracruz have incised carvings, originally filled with cinnabar, that depict gods and may identify the

wearer with the deity (Joralemon 1976). Olmec designs may have
extended over the whole body, and could have included figures or
repeated patterns created with ceramic stamps.

Ceramic masks from Chupícuaro, Guanajuato, are among the most
striking of Preclassic Mexico (cat. no. 20, illustrated). They were executed
in the Chupícuaro style, characterized by painted geometric decoration in
red, black, brown, and white. Stepfrets, crosses, and diamonds cover the
ceramic products of Chupícuaro, including figures of pregnant women
and hunchbacks (Weaver 1956; Natalie Wood ... 1969). These figurines
were part of a Mesoamerican tradition of female figurines, probably
related to human fertility, which flourished in the Preclassic and continued through the Colonial period. The decoration of the Chupícuaro figurines may have referred to face-painting, by either reproducing or
simplifying actual examples.

The style was retained in ceramic masks, but with more complex patterns and colors. These are true masks with the eyes and mouth pierced
through. No two masks bear identical designs, and although the
Chupícuaro figurines depict women, the complex face-painting depicted
on masks may have been restricted to men. If the designs represent the
face-painting of the wearer, these are generalized anthropomorphic portraits made specific by decoration. The example exhibited features a
repeating quadripartite design that encloses the eyes and mouth and
encircles the face (cat. no. 20, illustrated).

Among the Mixtecs and Aztecs, manuscripts and relief carvings indicate
that face-painting designs were associated with deities and rulers.
Although ceramic masks are rare, surviving Mixtec examples do show
face-painting much like that in preconquest manuscripts (cat. no. 21). In
addition, face-painting was translated into mosaics in Aztec and Mixtec
masks—mosaics in which the colors and designs of face-painting were
duplicated in tesserae made of exotic materials such as turquoise, coral,
and mother-of-pearl (cat. no. 55, cover). Like the brilliantly colored feathers of tropical birds that comprised the costumes accompanying these
masks, the face-painting was rendered in the most precious of materials.
At the burial of Mixtec rulers, the body was wrapped in layers of cotton
mantles, dressed in gold ornaments and a crown, and a mosaic mask was
placed over the face.

To Western eyes, the masks of Teotihuacán seem repetitive and
geometrized; however, this is in part the result of their deterioration over
time. Originally, they would have appeared extraordinarily lifelike, with
inlaid eyes of white shell, black irises of iron pyrite, and the mouths filled
with teeth of shell. Although the faces are rectangular, with conventionalized ears, the cheeks, lips, nose, and brow ridges are usually swelling vol-

umes whose organic qualities were brought out by the inlays (cat. no. 22). The stone would have appeared transformed into the face of a living being. Sometimes these masks had designs carved into the surface and inlaid with coral and turquoise. The addition of face-painting through paint or inlays would have created an impression of individuality which —when combined with a costume, as in a burial—would have secured the identity of the individual or at least his social role.

Representational portraits

Although some Olmec masks represent the Were-jaguar and other deities, the majority depict human faces. Most of the known, life-size stone masks are from an elite cemetery at Río Pesquero, Veracruz (cat. no. 19, illustrated). Although they are rectilinear with conventionalized ears, the modeling and apparent specificity of the features suggest that these are portraits, possibly of the ruler or lord with whose remains they were buried (Joralemon, in Parsons et al. 1988). The argument that these masks are representational can be made by analogy with Veracruz Monumental sculpture of the same area. The faces of these ceramic sculptures often have a marked individuality, and may have been portraits of members of the political and religious elite (Hammer 1971).

In Classic Veracruz, ceramic sculptures depict the use of helmet masks, but these were made of perishable materials. The only face masks preserved are those of aged persons, with sunken cheeks and deep lines around the eyes and mouth (cat. no. 26, illustrated).

A unique mask from the Virú culture of Peru shows an aged face with sharp features and deeply incised lines (cat. no. 27). The Tlatilco tradition includes masks that show aged faces, mustaches, beards, and other specific features.

In Peru, ceramic vessels of the Moche culture, which depict human heads, have long been recognized to include examples of "genuine portraits" (Donnan 1978, 3). Many must be classified as representational, while others are clearly idealized.

Although many masked figures are shown in Moche ceramic sculptures, only a few ceramic masks have been found. These are true masks with eyes and mouths pierced through; suspension holes indicate that they were worn. Like the portrait-head bottles, the features depicted on the face masks may represent specific individuals (cat. no. 29, illustrated). However, while the portrait bottles always show reserved, stereotyped expressions, the widely opened eyes and mouths of the masks are more than just functional, and give them an expressive quality not found in the bottles.

Face mask of old man
Classic Veracruz, Veracruz, Mexico
Classic, A.D. 600–900
ceramic, traces of paint
17.1 x 16.5 x 6.3 cm
Property from the collection of Edward and Nympha Montagu, Buffalo, New York
[CAT. NO. 26]

31

Although not a portrait, the same expressive quality appears in a deity mask with a sharp nose, feline fangs, and headdress ornaments including a feline face and lunette (cat. no. 28, illustrated). Such ornaments have been found in elite Moche burials. The mask must have served to identify its wearer with the deity depicted.

Emblematic portraits

Emblematic portraits were especially common in Peru and Central America, where costume and ornament served both to define and transform individuals. In Peru, deity attributes were depicted in both Paracas and Nazca textiles and in gold ornaments, which were apparently worn by both the living and the dead (cat. nos. 9, 10, illustrated). Mouth masks and forehead ornaments associated with the Oculate Being have been found in mummy bundles, over the faces of the deceased.

In Panama, gold plaques or pectorals depicting faces were worn by both the living and the dead (cat. no. 31, illustrated), and were, in a sense, emblematic portraits. Gold designated an elite group, and the embossings on these plaques—often zoomorphic representations—may have indicated the rank of warrior. They may also have been "property marks," identifying kinship and origin myths and branding personal belongings. Thus, these gold ornaments, alone, would have identified a person as a member of a clan or lineage group. The saurian pectoral shown may represent a crocodile or caiman (Cook and Bray 1985).

A Jama Coaque sculpture from Ecuador combines a mask, face-painting, elaborate headdress, and ritual or status paraphernalia in a single image (cat. no. 25, illustrated). The standing figure, attached to a vessel, wears a mask in the center of his headdress which duplicates his own face-painting. The headdress includes a fully modeled bird at the top, and the figure carries a baton and plays a set of panpipes. Thus, the mask in the headdress is a generalized anthropomorphic portrait, while the entire ensemble functions as an emblematic portrait of the individual.

Face mask
Olmec, Río Pesquero, Veracruz, Mexico
Preclassic, 900–600 B.C.
jade, burnt
17.1 x 15.2 cm
Honolulu Academy of Arts, Honolulu, Hawaii
[CAT. NO. 19]

Pectoral with feline face
Macaracas, Sitio Conte, Panama, excavated by S. K. Lothrop
Period V–VI, A.D. 500–1100
gold
9.5 x 10 cm
The Cleveland Museum of Art, Cleveland, Ohio
[CAT. NO. 31]

Face mask with geometric designs
Chupícuaro, Guanajuato, Mexico
Late Preclassic, 500–100 B.C.
ceramic, paint
19.3 x 17.4 x 2.5 cm
National Museum of the American Indian,
Smithsonian Institution, New York, New York
[CAT. NO. 20]

*Figure wearing headdress
with bird and central mask,
holding rattle and panpipes*
Jama Coaque, Ecuador
Regional Developmental, 500
B.C.–A.D. 500
ceramic, black paint
27.3 x 15.2 x 27.9 cm
Museo Antropológico, Banco
Central de Ecuador, Guayaquil,
Ecuador
[CAT. NO. 25]

◆
*Face mask with headdress
with half-moon, feline
decorations and circular
earrings*
Moche, North Coast, Peru
Early Intermediate, 200
B.C.–A.D. 600
ceramic
18.9 x 18.1 cm
Museo Nacional de Arqueología
y Antropología, Lima, Peru
[CAT. NO. 28]

***Face mask with knotted
headdress with feline
ornament***
Moche, North Coast, Peru
Early Intermediate, 200 B.C.–A.D.
600
ceramic
19.5 x 16.5 cm
Museo Nacional de Arqueología
y Antropología, Lima, Peru

[CAT. NO. 29]

***Face mask with lower half
painted red***
Michoacán, Mexico
Postclassic, A.D. 1200–1500
ceramic, paint, copper
15.4 x 14.5 x 4 cm
National Museum of the
American Indian, Smithsonian
Institution, New York,
New York

[CAT. NO.30]

***Mask with serrated
crest and painted
designs***
Playa Venado, Panama,
excavated by Neville A. Hart
Period V, A.D. 500–1000
ceramic, paint
25.5 x 24 x 13 cm
Peabody Museum of
Archaeology and Ethnology,
Harvard University, Cam-
bridge, Massachusetts

[CAT. NO. 32]

BURIAL AND
SUBSTITUTION

The SUBSTITUTION OF MASKS for human faces is often found in burials of the elite. In Peru, especially, masks were an important element in the assemblage of costume, jewelry, ceramics, and other objects that furnished tombs and adorned the bodies of the deceased. These objects recreated the living world of the elite and identified their social position in it, both iconographically and materially.

Masks placed directly on the faces of corpses are the clearest examples of substitution, although they also, of course, represent transformation. If he was a shaman, the dead individual might be transformed into the supernatural being who was his spirit helper during life. Or, the individual might be transformed into the supernatural figure who was important to him through dynastic or other contexts, such as the Aztec military orders, where ideas of transformation of humans into anthropomorphic or zoomorphic supernaturals were incorporated. While many sorts of masks may be transformational, those that depict the human face after death also substitute for the decayed flesh of the corpse.

Among the Inca, the use of burial masks is not known. Their rulers were preserved as mummies whose bodies, carried on litters in public ceremonies, continued to serve as a focus for the economic and political power of their families and retainers. (This system may have originated at Chan Chan, the Chimú capital, which has nine palaces centered around tombs.)

Beginning in the first half of the fifteenth century A.D., the Peruvian area and beyond was united by the Inca into a tribute empire, Tawantin-suyu. However, local burial practices continued to be followed in the conquered regions, including burial in masked mortuary bundles.

There are many examples of substitution on the Peruvian coast, where the dry climate has preserved much of the complement of funeral goods created by the Paracas, Nazca, Huari, and other cultures. In the Paracas and Nazca cemeteries on the Paracas peninsula, mummy bundles were created by wrapping a multitude of textiles around the body of the deceased. The bundles included mantles and other clothing elaborately decorated with woven, embroidered, or painted images; plain weave textiles separated the layers of decorated cloth and formed the outer layers of the bundle, which was then covered with a mat of woven reeds. Within the bundle, the body was usually placed in a flexed, seated position. It was sometimes treated to make it less subject to decay by drying or smoking and by covering it with a chemical substance like bitumen; the primary preservative, however, was the dry coastal climate itself.

Included in the bundles were objects worn in life, such as gold mouth masks, forehead ornaments, animal skins, caps, and loincloths. In some examples, a veritable substitution took place within the mummy bundle, where a ceramic vessel replaced the human head. This may have been done to replace heads lost as trophies in warfare (Proulx 1971).

The mortuary bundle became a substitute for the entire body of the deceased when it was anthropomorphized by the addition of a large mask or an entire false head. The earliest example of this is from the Paracas culture in the Ica Valley, where cloth squares backed with unspun cotton pads were attached near the tops of the mortuary bundles. Painted on these squares are the face—and in later times the entire body—of the Oculate Being (Dawson 1979). A long fringe of unwoven yarn across the top of these squares represents hair and was draped over the top of the bundle to the back.

This practice spread in the Middle Horizon (A.D. 550–950), when the expansionist state centered at the city of Huari, Ayacucho, controlled much of highland and coastal Peru. The artistic style of the Middle Horizon was angular and prismatic, with striking juxtapositions of colors; the iconography and decorative motifs originated at Tiwanaku, Bolivia.

The false heads and masks added to the bundles are much larger than the human head or face. The mummy bundles stand four or more feet in height; if the anthropomorphized bundle is analogous to a seated human being, then the larger than life-size masks and false heads are scaled to the proportions of the bundles. The masks and heads lack recognizable deity attributes; rather, the ornaments or face-painting may duplicate those of the individual in life.

The false heads for mortuary bundles were made somewhat like pillows: plain weave cotton textiles were wrapped around reeds and leaves, then bound with cotton cord. The faces could be created in one of two ways:

by using a textile as the ground or base for a painting or attached objects; or by adding a separately carved and painted wooden face or mask.

When the textile served as the ground, the facial features could be painted directly on it; usually a textile of finer quality was used, then attached to the coarser stuffed head. Alternatively, objects of metal, shell, cloth, hair, or feathers could be sewn on the textile. Faces created with feather mosaic are the most colorful and striking examples of attached objects. Feather mosaic mantles and hangings were made by sewing the feathers to textiles in overlapping layers, but the stiff filling of reeds and leaves inside the false head made it necessary to attach the feathers for the mosaic with an adhesive with almost no overlapping.

Carved wooden faces for false heads may show only the face or, as in the case of the two exhibited examples (cat. nos. 37, 38), may be at the center of a plaque. The plaque could serve as the base for attached hair and ornaments, or the surface could be used as the ground for painted depictions of ornaments such as necklaces and headdresses. The face panels exhibited are in the Middle Horizon style of the Huara Valley, a localized and simplified version of Huari style (Sawyer 1975).

The Middle Sicán culture of the north coast of Peru (A.D. 850–1050) also created mummy bundles, decorated with large gold masks. Like the heads made for the Huari bundles, these masks were scaled to the proportions of the bundle rather than the body inside. Another parallel to Huari is the use of feather mosaics; much of the face was painted red with cinnabar, but the unpainted areas sometimes show the remains of feathers pasted to the surface in varicolored mosaic patterns.

The Middle Sicán masks are sheets of gold with the facial features created in low relief by hammering, probably over wooden forms. They typically have slanted, teardrop eyes, an oval mouth, and a projecting nose (sometimes formed of a separate sheet of metal) within a rectangular face. The mask swells toward the center, but deeply impressed lines set off the cheeks from a flattened area around the mouth. The entire mask curves to fit the exterior surface of the mummy bundle. The masks are decorated with oversized ornaments, including large earspools. The gold, copper, and stone ornaments that hang from the nose, mouth, ears, and below the chin straps were surely worn, in smaller versions, by the elite individuals within the bundles.

The masks may represent a deity or idealized ruler. This face is depicted on a variety of grave goods, including hammered metal beakers, ceramics, and wood sculptures. The colorful paint, feather mosaics, and the motile, dangling ornaments would seem almost to revivify the deceased, and the placing of this mask on the bundle appears to identify the elite dead with the deity or ruler (Shimada 1985).

Face mask
Late Intrusive Woodlands, Heinish
Mound, Scioto County, Ohio
Woodlands, 1000 B.C.–A.D. 500
stone
15 x 11 x 8 cm
Ohio Historical Society, Columbus,
Ohio
[CAT. NO. 43]

The making of false heads for mortuary bundles continued on the central coast of Peru in the Late Intermediate Period (A.D. 1000–1476), when the region was divided into small polities extending over one or two valleys. The Chancay Valley region is notable for the great quantity of funerary offerings found in its sizable cemeteries, especially open weave textiles or gauzes (usually featuring geometric and zoomorphic designs), and white ceramics decorated with minimal linear painting in black and red (Sawyer 1975, 129–164). Chancay false heads consist of painted wooden faces, human hair, metal ornaments such as headbands and hairpins, and head-covering cloths (also found as grave offerings) (cat. no. 41).

The Chancay culture also made genuine face masks. One painted ceramic example which is life-sized, could have been used to cover a human face (cat. no. 42, illustrated). Chancay ceramic figures and effigy jars, depicting men and women, show face-painting like that of the mask; as in the Chupícuaro style, the patterns on the masks are far more complex than on the sculptures.

These mummy heads and masks of wood, cloth, and metal supplanted the human face with the materials that would outlast it. In the dry desert climate of coastal Peru, these materials, which we usually think of as perishable, became imperishable substitutes for the human face.

In Mesoamerica, substitution of a mask for the human face was achieved primarily in stone, less frequently in ceramics. Masks found in burials, covering the face of the deceased (such as those from the tombs of Mayan rulers like King Pacal), were permanent replacements for the features that would be lost to decay. For the elite Olmec of Río Pesquero, stone masks replaced the faces. Ceramic masks may have replaced those on the groups of bodies in West Mexican tombs.

For the most part, the tombs of Mesoamerica were designed to be sealed after a single use, but in West Mexico, the great shaft-and-chamber tombs housed many burials. The bodies, laid out in what was probably a concentric circle at the center of the chamber, could be seen at each reopening, including the ceramic masks over their faces (cat. no. 3) (cat. no.4, illustrated).

In the eastern United States, the use of funerary masks may have begun in the Late Woodlands period (A.D. 500–1000). A stone mask from southern Ohio, carved from a single piece of stone, is recorded from a Late Woodlands burial (Mills 1922, 566) (cat. no. 43, illustrated). Like two similar, unprovenanced works (in the Ross County Historical Society and Cincinnati Art Museum), the eyes and mouth are not pierced through.

During the Mississippian Period (A.D. 1000–1600), major sites like Spiro, Oklahoma; Moundville, Alabama; and Etowah, Georgia, were composed of plazas and large earthen platforms topped by architectural structures.

Some of these served as mortuary temples dedicated to the ancestors of the elite. They housed the remains of the highest level of society, as well as a variety of mortuary and memorial objects including wooden figures, face masks, and maskettes. The face masks were not meant to be worn by the living, for most had inlaid shell eyes. The maskettes functioned as small equivalents for the funerary masks (cat. no. 77).

During both the Late Woodlands and Mississippian periods, secondary burial was practiced by the elite, who transferred the bones of ancestors to new graves or mortuary temples. Masks and maskettes of wood, shell, and stone perpetuated the appearance of the dead, and legitimized the power of the living.

False head for mortuary bundle
Pachacamac, Peru
Middle Horizon–Late Intermediate,
A.D. 800–1200
wood with shell inlays, textiles, feathers
27 x 19 cm
American Museum of Natural History,
New York, New York
[CAT. NO. 35]

False head for mortuary bundle
Huari, Central Coast, Peru
Middle Horizon, A.D. 600–1000
textiles, feathers, reeds
38.1 x 25.4 x 17.7 cm
Collection of Arthur G. Rosen, New Jersey
[CAT. NO. 36]

Mask
Sicán, North Coast, Peru
Late Intermediate, Middle Sicán, A.D. 850–1050
gold
23.5 x 51 cm
Museo Arqueológico Regional Bruning, Lambayeque, Peru
[CAT. NO. 39]

Mask
Sicán, North Coast, Peru
Late Intermediate, Middle Sican, A.D. 850–1050
gold
19.5 x 32.2 cm
Museo Arqueológico Regional Bruning, Lambayeque, Peru
[CAT. NO. 40]

*Face mask with geometric
decoration and parallel lines crossing the face*
Chancay, Central Coast, Peru
Late Intermediate, A.D. 1100–1400
ceramic, white with red and black paint, fabric ties in
suspension holes
18 x 15.5 cm
Museo Amano, Miraflores, Peru
[CAT. NO. 42]

STATE-LEVEL SOCIETIES

STATE-LEVEL SOCIETIES in Pre-Columbian America incorporated masks in a variety of public ceremonies. The Aztec emperor wore masks and costumes of the deities on state and festival occasions. Soldiers of the Mesoamerican states wore helmet masks and costumes not only in ceremonial contexts, but also in battle. Priests wore masks and costumes during festivals and religious rites. Masks were important elements in the panoply of display that served to legitimize the rule of the state.

In the Aztec empire—a tributary state based on military conquest—masks were items of tribute. They were rendered both as completed objects and in their constituent parts (tesserae of turquoise and other rare materials), which presumably were assembled in the Aztec capital by resident artisans (Klein 1980).

The best known types of Aztec masks that have been preserved are stone and turquoise mosaic face masks (Carmichael 1970). Although few mosaic masks survive, many stone masks were uncovered in the excavations of the Aztec Templo Mayor in 1978–80. These masks may have been rendered as tribute; they represent a number of styles, and some have painted glyphs on their reverse side that may indicate their origins. One, in the style of the much earlier Teotihuacán culture, is probably an Aztec copy of originals from the site (where the Aztecs believed the gods had been born) (Pasztory 1987, 452–453, n.1). It is unlikely that these masks were either worn or placed on statues. Rather, their burial as offerings at the Templo Mayor probably symbolized the right of the Aztec state to collect tribute from conquered populations, and to offer it to the deities honored in their temples: Huitzilopochtli, the Aztecs' own warlike patron, and Tlaloc, the old Mesoamerican god of rain (Klein 1986).

An important achievement of the imperial system was the revaluation and reinterpretation of past Mesoamerican religious practices to legitimize the Aztec state. For example, a major Mesoamerican festival marking the beginning of the rainy season was Tlacaxipehualiztli, which honored the deity Xipe Totec. At this time of year, sacrificial victims were flayed and their skins worn by impersonators of the deity, whose blessings ensured human and agricultural fertility in the coming year (cat. no. 59, illustrated). In the Aztec state, it became the primary festival celebrating the military accomplishments of the soldiers who carried out the imperial conquests (Broda 1970). Flayed skin masks were made by the Aztecs as trophies of successful military engagements, and masks also were made from the skulls of sacrificed captives (Klein 1986). A beautifully modeled Aztec mask may be a representation in ceramic of a mask made from the facial skin of a captive (cat. no. 45, illustrated).

The *pochteca*, or merchant class of the Aztec empire, served as the advance guard for conquest of new territories. Much of the Huastec region of the Gulf Coast of Mexico was conquered by the Aztecs, which may be reflected in a Huastec mask of the patron deity of merchants (cat. no. 46, illustrated).

The Mixtec region lies to the south of the center of the Aztec empire, in the modern states of Oaxaca and Puebla. The city-states of this region, ruled by kings who could trace their ancestry back to the tenth century A.D. using pictorial genealogies, were centers for the production of small-scale works of art. These were precious and highly portable objects that were widely traded by the elites of the surrounding regions. For at least the last four decades before the Spanish Conquest, most of this area was controlled by the Aztec empire and had a profound impact on Aztec imperial arts.

A group of turquoise mosaic masks, discovered in a cave in Puebla, provides a look at a major art form that influenced the Aztecs (cat. no. 55, illustrated). These masks do not have deity attributes; rather, they seem close to images of the elite in Mixtec genealogical manuscripts. Saville suggested they were used in ceremonials until relatively recently; the mask exhibited had been repaired in the broken mouth area with a piece of tin (Saville 1922, 47–67). However, they may have come from burials in a cave at Peña de Ejutla. The forty-five chambers in this cave were tombs for local Mixtec or Cuicatec rulers and nobles, who were wrapped in textiles and sealed with offerings in rooms built in the cave (Moser 1983). In Mixtec genealogical manuscripts, rulers appear in different scenes wearing various kinds of face-painting and masks. Possibly Mixtec nobles, like Aztec emperors, were buried with groups of nobles.

Olmec rulers also may have owned groups of masks. The variety of

Mask of the Merchant God
Huastec, Veracruz, Mexico
Postclassic, A.D. 1200–1500
gray ceramic, black paint
12.7 x 11.4 x 6.3 cm
Hudson Museum, University of Maine, Orono, Maine
[CAT. NO. 46]

Olmec masks in stone—from portraits to extraordinary deity images, found at Río Pesquero and throughout Mesoamerica—suggests the kings had masks emblematic of their political and religious roles. Masks of the Were-Jaguar, which probably was the god of rain, could have symbolized an Olmec king's role as intermediary between his community and the supernatural world (cat. no. 48). The suggestion that a single individual could be associated with multiple deities seems to be supported by the famous Las Limas figurine, a stone carving of a seated figure on whose body are incised the faces of four deities while in its lap it holds a fifth Were-Jaguar in the form of a child (Joralemon 1976).

Masks were an important element in the symbolism of state at Teotihuacán. This city, founded before A.D. 1, created a state-level society that concentrated almost the entire population of the Basin of Mexico in a single urban complex. It was built on a grid plan, composed almost entirely of closed, inward-looking apartment compounds decorated with polychromatic murals on plaster walls. Each compound was centered on a patio, probably for ceremonial activities for the groups that lived there. The existence of about twenty complexes, each composed of three temples arranged to define a rectangular courtyard open at one end, suggests that the city was divided into districts. The courtyards of these three-temple complexes must have provided settings for rituals for the entire ward. The images on the murals of the apartment compounds, and painted on polychromatic frescoed vessels, show figures wearing helmet masks and elaborate zoomorphic and avian headdresses. Since these were made of perishable materials, none survive, but the painted images of figures in processions and engaging in ritual activities probably show how such masks appeared in Teotihuacán's ceremonial spaces.

The figures in the murals appear to be composed of a limited number of conventionalized and geometricized components, assembled in various combinations to form different images. Ceramic incensarios were in fact made this way. A superstructure comprising as many as two dozen molded parts was placed on an hourglass-shaped base; at the center was a miniature mask, recessed and surrounded by symbols forming a rectangular frame (cat. no. 50) (Berlo 1982).

Stone and ceramic masks in the Teotihuacán style are the most numerous type of mask remaining from any Pre-Columbian culture (cat. nos. 22, 33, 50–52, 62, 63). Few have been found in controlled excavations, and their uses remain uncertain. A ceramic model of a figure with a separately made mask attached at the top was excavated from a child's burial at Teotihuacán; it may show how the life-sized or larger masks were used (*Mexico...* 1990, 98–99).

Face masks and elaborate headdresses were worn by and buried with Mayan rulers and other members of the elite. Extant Mayan masks are primarily funerary in function: jade mosaic masks that covered the faces of rulers in their tombs; solid jade masks with inlaid eyes and mouth, depicting deities; and rare ceramic masks in the Jaina Island style, probably from burials containing the elaborate ceramic figurines for which this area is known (cat. no. 53, illustrated). Miniature masks in jade and other stones formed part of the costumes of rulers, worn on headdresses, collars and belts.

In the Andean region, the use of masks to reinforce the legitimacy of rulers was apparently less extensive than in Mesoamerica. Masks from the Early Horizon are rare, but at least one true mask in bone in the Chavín style has been found on the north coast of Peru (Segundo Vásquez Sánchez, personal communication, 1991). Coastal burials of the Middle Horizon have yielded few masks that could be worn by a living person. False heads and larger than life-sized gold masks, clearly designed to be attached to mortuary bundles, designated the elite in death, but could not have been used in life (Willey 1971, 163, fig. 3–98).

In the eastern United States, masks were a part of the paraphernalia of power for the rulers and warriors of major centers in the Mississippian period. Shell carvings from Spiro and elsewhere show armed figures, sometimes with trophy heads, wearing masks and winged costumes of birds of prey. Some shell masks with falcon markings on the eyes are known. However, pierced face masks were far outnumbered by mortuary masks and masklike objects of shell or metal worn as gorgets, ear ornaments, and decorations on headdresses. Such mask ornaments depict human faces, falcons, deer, and the Long-Nosed-God (cat. no. 77) (cat. no. 78, illustrated).

When Cortés first entered Tenochtitlan, the last Aztec emperor, Mocteuczoma Xocoyotl, presented him with—among other gifts—a set of royal turquoise mosaic masks depicting deities. This marked the end of the use of masks for the purposes of the state in Central Mexico, where it reached its highest development in the Americas.

Face mask
Aztec, Valley of Mexico
Postclassic, A.D. 1300–1521
ceramic
18.4 cm
American Museum of Natural History,
New York, New York
[CAT. NO. 45]

Mask of were–jaguar
Olmec, Mexico
Preclassic, 900–600 B.C.
stone
14.6 x 12 x 6.3 cm
Mexican Museum, San Francisco,
California
[CAT. NO. 48]

**Mold-made mask with glyph
8 Ahau on forehead**
Maya, Jaina style, Guaymil,
Campeche, Mexico
Late Classic, A.D. 550–950
ceramic, paint
15.5 x 12.6 x 6.5 cm
National Museum of the American
Indian, Smithsonian Institution,
New York, New York
[CAT. NO. 53]

ARCHITECTURE

THERE WERE TWO principal uses of masks in Pre-Columbian architecture. First, monumental masks were often integral parts of architectural facades. Second, large-scale images of masked human figures or deities also were used in architectural contexts. (It is possible that stone or metal masks in life-sized or larger scale were not intended to be worn, but were designed to be placed on a statue or structure as architectural objects.)

In Mesoamerica, pyramids were conceived of as symbolic sacred mountains, and they were surrounded by sculptural ensembles having religious significance. In early Mayan structures at Uaxactun, Nakbe, Acanceh, and other sites, monumental plaster masks were attached to stairways and building facades. In Classic period temples, great stucco masks were placed on facades and roofs at sites like Piedras Negras and Copán.

Three architectural styles of the Late Classic period feature the most elaborate use of architectural masks found in the Americas. The Puuc, Río Bec, and Chenes styles developed in the Yucatan peninsula of Mexico. At the Puuc site of Labná, entire facades of buildings are composed of repeating, monumental serpent masks. At Uxmal, the stairs of the largest structure, the Pyramid of the Magician, is lined with masks, and the structure is topped by a single, immense mask. The Chenes style features facades composed of masks in stone mosaic, while in Río Bec-style buildings masks are more clearly grouped and separated by other architectural elements (Kubler 1984, 267–70).

In Central Mexico, the architectural use of masks never approaches that of the Mayan region. An exception is the Pyramid of Quetzalcoatl at Teotihuacán, the facade of which is covered with masks of a saurian creature with rings on his forehead and heads of the Feathered Serpent. However,

54

Mask with holes for inlays and suspension
Teotihuacán style, found in Tlatelolco, Mexico
Middle Classic, A.D. 300–750
greenstone
27 x 31.5 x 15 cm
National Museum of the American Indian, Smithsonian Institution, New York, New York

[CAT. NO. 62]

in Central and Western Mexico, and in Veracruz, the ceremonial complex at the heart of each community was an ensemble of buildings and sculptures that included masked sculptures (Heyden and Gendrop 1973). Figures of Xipe Totec, for example, were made in stone and ceramic by Toltec, Aztec, and Huastec sculptors (cat. no. 59, illustrated).

Approaching pyramids or entering symbolic caves between masks or through the open mouths of deities clearly identifies the structure with deities of mountains or caves. This visual metaphor continues to the final periods of Mesoamerican architecture, as in the great maw around the doorway at the Aztec temple cut into the living rock at Malinalco (Markman and Markman 1989, 82–87).

A crested stone head, hollow and drilled with suspension holes at the top, was found at the Pyramid of the Niches at El Tajín, Veracruz (cat. no. 61, illustrated) (cf. Proskouriakoff 1971, 565–68). Now dissociated from its original architectural context, it may have been an element of the facade or served as the face of a statue.

Teotihuacán stone masks may have been funerary objects, but they must also have been architectural elements. They could have served as the faces of sculptures made of wood, dressed in costumes to create busts or figures like those seen in the murals of the city. Such figures might have been life-sized, like the majority of the stone masks, but there are also masks that are several times life-size, which could have served as the faces of truly massive and impressive figures (cat. nos. 62, 63, illustrated). The masks certainly had ornaments in the holes drilled in the ears, and might have had face-painting or nose or mouth ornaments. Such figures would have been part of the sculptural and architectural ensemble of public ritual spaces, like later Toltec and Aztec stone sculptures. These figures could have been "dressed differently for seasonal rites or for different status or occupation groups [and] may have been some of the most highly valued and venerated ritual images at Teotihuacán" (Pasztory 1988, 64).

The Tarascan kingdom of Michoacán was never conquered by the Aztecs, but its public spaces were decorated—like Aztec pyramids and plazas—with ensembles of stone sculpture depicting deities and military figures. The buildings themselves had relatively limited decoration, primarily small relief carvings of floral and geometric designs. Rulers were buried in turquoise mosaic masks (Craine and Reindorp 1970). Large masks of volcanic stone might also have been funerary objects, but they are larger than life-size, and could have formed part of sculptural and architectural groupings, either suspended on building walls or as the faces of statues (cat. no. 66).

All West Mexican tomb sculpture was designed ultimately for use in the architectural context of the shaft-and-chamber tombs that were excavated under the round buildings at the heart of many of the sites. Phil C. Weigand (personal communication, 1991) has suggested that before being placed in tombs, the larger examples of tomb sculptures were used as architectural decorations for the houses over these round structures (cat. no. 6, illustrated). The round courtyards surrounded by houses on platforms were ideal settings for such sculptures (Couch 1988).

In the Andean region, an interesting characteristic of the earliest periods of architecture—particularly the Early Horizon along the north coast—is the use of large masks and adobe figures on facades. At sites like Punkurí, in the Nepeña Valley, and Moxeke, in the Moxeke Valley, the stairways and entrances to public buildings were flanked by such brightly painted adobe sculptures in high relief. These types of decoration disappear after the Early Horizon and are not seen again.

Statue of Ehecatl, God of the Wind
Veracruz, Mexico
Postclassic, A.D. 900–1200
ceramic
78 x 40 x 24 cm
Hudson Museum, University of Maine,
Orono, Maine
[CAT. NO. 60]

Statue of Xipe Totec
Huastec or Aztec, Veracruz, Mexico
Postclassic, A.D. 1200–1500
ceramic
133.9 x 39.3 x 35.5 cm
Hudson Museum, University of Maine,
Orono, Maine
[CAT. NO. 59]

57

Mask with fanged mouth
Central Mexico
Colonial, 16th–18th Century
stone with traces of red and green stucco
25.5 x 23 x 13 cm
National Museum of the American Indian,
Smithsonian Institution, New York, New York

[CAT. NO. 63]

Hollow crested human head with
suspension holes
Classic Veracruz, Pyramid of the Niches, El Tajín,
Veracruz, Mexico
Classic, A.D. 600–900
scoria
23.5 x 14 x 15.5 cm
National Museum of the American Indian, Smithsonian
Institution, New York, New York

[CAT. NO. 61]

59

Mask
Sicán, North Coast, Peru
Late Intermediate, Middle Sicán,
A.D. 850–1050
gold
26 x 47.6 x 7.6 cm
M. Ulloa Collection
[CAT. NO. 68]

Mask
Mixtec, Oaxaca or Puebla, Mexico
Postclassic, A.D. 1200–1500
gray stone
15.5 x 14 cm
Honolulu Academy of Arts, Honolulu, Hawaii
[CAT. NO. 64]

RITUAL PERFORMANCE

MANY MASKS cannot be understood outside the context of masking, where they are worn in dances or ceremonies enacted for an audience. In the Pre-Columbian experience, the actors and audience would have included the elite, commoners, and persons—such as priests—who had expert knowledge of the conceptual basis for both masks and ceremonies.

The evidence for preconquest masking is, of course, indirect, and rather scanty. Spanish documents of the contact period describe masks in use at public festivals as well as in ceremonies performed in more elite and exclusive contexts. The best-documented performances are those of the Aztec, Mixtec, and other Mesoamerican peoples. The accounts of Spanish missionaries, who recorded the festival cycle of Central Mexico, have served as a basis for reconstructing ceremonies from even the earliest periods.

For cultures without written records, painting, sculpture, and the architectural complexes that served as ritual spaces may yield information about the uses of masks and costumes. The study of architecture and its ceremonial use offers the most promising avenue for the understanding of ritual. Ultimately, however, most history of Pre-Columbian masking cannot be recovered.

One of the most widespread and best-documented performances in Mesoamerica was the ball game. From unknown origins in the Formative period, through its greatest flourishing in the Classic period, until the conquest and, in the far west of Mexico, until this century, the ball game was a major focus of public ritual. In the Classic period, the Veracruz coastal regions were a major avenue of trade between Teotihuacán in Central Mexico and the Mayan area; in addition to its religious significance

Cast of wooden face mask
Calusa, Key Marco, Forida
Late Mississippian, A.D.1400–1500
plaster copy of original wood, with
paint, shell inlays in eyes
26 x 14 x 8.5 cm
Mrs. Marion Gilliland, Gainesville,
Florida
[CAT. NO. 75]

(attested by cosmological and agricultural imagery in the ball courts), the ball games probably served as an occasion for markets and peaceful trading. The relief carvings on ball courts from El Tajín, Veracruz, and Chichén Itzá, Yucatan, indicate that ballplayers wore elaborate costumes, often including helmet masks. Ball game equipment, such as *hachas* (axes), also depicts masks over the faces of ballplayers and deities.

The ball game was also played in the Caribbean, where Taino ballplayers may have worn small stone maskettes as part of their equipment (cat. no. 71). These small, oval, stone objects may be the only remaining reflection of the Caribbean mask-making tradition of the contact period (Ekholm 1961; Fewkes 1913).

Offerings of figurines may also yield information about ritual performance and masking. In Mesoamerica, graves were often richly furnished with ceramic or stone figurines, especially in the Preclassic period. Groups of nearly identical figurines were probably not portraits of or companions for the dead, but may have represented groups that danced at festivals or at occaions such as funerals or marriages (Scott 1987). Female figurines with face- and body-painting, such as those from Chupícaro and Tlatilco, might represent dancers for human and agricultural fertility. Olmec figurines, in ritual groupings, have been found in offerings and burials (Coe 1968). Stone figurines with Were-jaguar faces may be wearing masks (cf. cat. nos. 15 and 48, illustrated); few have been recovered archaeologically, but they may have been part of ritual groupings.

Among the most elaborate Mesoamerican figurines are those made by the cultures of Classic Veracruz (cf. cat. nos. 7, 26 illustrated). These figurines depict many types of masks and costumes, including helmet masks which were made separately and could be removed from the figurines (this type of figurine was also made by the Maya). One remarkable funerary offering consisted of twleve helmet masks without figurines, each of a different type, placed on sticks and arranged in a circle around the deceased (cat. no. 81, illustrated).

Preserved in the mud of the Florida swamps was a rich body of wooden artifacts at the Mississippian site of Key Marco, including eight complete face masks (cat. no. 74) (cat. no. 75, illustrated). Most are carved from a single piece of wood and are slightly hollowed in back, making it possible that they were worn over the face. Many are painted with facial markings, perhaps to represent animals or deities. Some have the eyes pierced through, and in three curious instances, eyes of two different sizes appear on the same mask. Also found at the Key Marco site were a number of hollow, three-dimensional figureheads depicting animals, which could have been worn on headdresses.

The masks were almost certainly used in a ceremonial context, and, in fact, the entire Key Marco site—which consists of a series of shell mounds—is thought to have been a ceremonial center. The exploitation of the area's rich marine and lacustrine resources permitted the development of a sedentary, stratified society, among whom sophisticated craftsmanship indicates the presence of specialized artisans. The abandonment of the Key Marco site, probably occurring between A.D. 1400 and 1500, remains mysterious. Judging by the wealth of beautiful and finely crafted objects left behind, it appears to have been sudden and involuntary (Gilliland 1988, 1989).

Woodlands masking of the Mississippian period (A.D. 1000–1600) has left a record engraved in shells and embossed on copper plates showing figures dancing, often in elaborate birdman costumes; playing chunkey (a type of ball game); riding in litters; and taking or displaying trophy heads. Some shell masks are engraved with markings around the eyes, suggesting that they formed parts of costumes depicting predatory birds. Most apparent masks are actually shell gorgets or other ornaments, the wearing of which is also illustrated in scenes engraved on shells (cat. no. 78, illustrated) (Brose et al. 1985).

In South America, the Tuza Ceramic Complex of the Nariño region of Colombia (A.D. 1250–1500) should probably be associated with the Pastos. This highly organized society, governed by a single ruler, had a powerful merchant class. One trade item was coca leaf, and a particularly rare mask shows a coca chewer with one cheek balled out (Labbé 1986, 133–34; pl. 48, p. 189). An erotic mask that may have played a role in fertility ceremonies features a line of four phallic figurines seated across the top of a woven headband (cat. no. 73, illustrated).

In Venezuela, the cemetery of Quibor has yielded very rich burials furnished with beautiful objects, including ceramic masks (Delgado R. and Molina 1983). Most are pierced through the eyes and mouth, hence made to be worn in life. Many are musical instruments as well; the open mouths have projecting lips that alter and amplify the song or speech of the wearer. The unique mask exhibited here has the eyes pierced through, but the rectangular mouth is not pierced (cat. no. 79, illustrated). The incised teeth suggest a skull, and, rather than having been worn, the mask may have been attached to a figure of wood or textiles by the perforation holes that ring its perimeter (Arroyo C. et al. 1971, 142).

Face mask with four phallic figures on headdress
Nariño, Colombia
Late period, Tuza Ceramic Complex, A.D. 1250–1500
ceramic with paint
32 x 17.7 x 4.5 cm
Dr. Stephen Blair, Newport Beach, Californi
[CAT. NO. 73]

Shell gorget of human face painted red
Cross County, Arkansas
Mississippian, A.D. 1200–1500
shell with red paint
11.5 x 10 x 2.3 cm
National Museum of the American Indian,
Smithsonian Institution, New York, New York

[CAT. NO. 78]

*Rectangular face mask with eyes
pierced through*
Cementerio de Quibor, Venezuela
Late, A.D. 300–1000
ceramic
13.3 x 15.2 x 2.5 cm
Collection of Harry and Maxula Mannil, Caracas,
Venezuela

[CAT. NO. 79]

Face mask
Vicús, Piura Region, North Peru
A.D. 100–800
ceramic, with white painted stripes
29 x 30 cm
Museo Arqueológico Rafael Larco
Herrera, Lima, Peru

[CAT. NO. 80]

Seven miniature helmet masks
Nopiloa, Classic Veracruz, Veracruz, Mexico
Classic, A.D. 600–900
ceramic with black asphalt paint
A. 23/3513 8 x 6.5 x 6.5 cm;
B. 23/3514 6.5 x 6.7 x 6.5 cm;
C. 23/3515 7 x 7.2 x 6.6 cm;
D. 23/3516 7 x 6.3 x 8 cm;
E. 23/3517 8 x 7.1 x 10.5 cm;
F. 23/3518 7.3 x 6 x 6.5 cm;
G. 23/3519 9.8 x 6.5 x 7 cm
National Museum of the American
Indian, Smithsonian Institution,
New York, New York

[CAT. NO. 81]

Pectoral of feline face for kuraka's dance costume
Trujillo Region, North Coast, Peru
Colonial, 17th–18th Century
gold, repoussé
25 x 33 x 3.1 cm
Krannert Art Museum and Kinkead Pavilion, University of
Illinois at Champaign-Urbana, Illinois

[CAT. NO. 18]

LENDERS TO THE EXHIBITION

AMERICAN MUSEUM OF NATURAL HISTORY, NEW YORK, NEW YORK

THE BALTIMORE MUSEUM OF ART, BALTIMORE, MARYLAND

BIRMINGHAM MUSEUM OF ART, BIRMINGHAM, ALABAMA

DR. STEPHEN BLAIR, NEWPORT BEACH, CALIFORNIA

BOWERS MUSEUM, SANTA ANA, CALIFORNIA

COLLECTION OF HARRY AND MAXULA MANNIL, CARACAS, VENEZUELA,

COLLECTION OF MR. AND MRS. LUIS NABOA, NEW YORK

COLLECTION OF ARTHUR G. ROSEN, NEW JERSEY

THE CLEVELAND MUSEUM OF ART, CLEVELAND, OHIO

MRS. MARION GILLILAND, GAINESVILLE, FLORIDA

HONOLULU ACADEMY OF ARTS, HONOLULU, HAWAII

HOUSTON MUSEUM OF FINE ARTS, HOUSTON, TEXAS

HUDSON MUSEUM, UNIVERSITY OF MAINE, ORONO, MAINE

KRANNERT ART MUSEUM AND KINKEAD PAVILION, UNIVERSITY OF ILLINOIS
AT CHAMPAIGN-URBANA, ILLINOIS

MEXICAN MUSEUM, SAN FRANCISCO, CALIFORNIA

MUSEO AMANO, MIRAFLORES, PERU

MUSEO ANTROPOLÓGICO, BANCO CENTRAL DE ECUADOR, GUAYAQUIL, ECUADOR

MUSEO NACIONAL DE ARQUEOLOGÍA Y ANTROPOLOGÍA, LIMA, PERU

MUSEO ARQUEOLÓGICO RAFAEL LARCO HERRERA, LIMA, PERU

MUSEO ARQUEOLÓGICO REGIONAL BRUNING, LAMBAYEQUE, PERU

NATIONAL MUSEUM OF THE AMERICAN INDIAN, SMITHSONIAN INSTITUTION,
NEW YORK, NEW YORK

OHIO HISTORICAL SOCIETY, COLUMBUS, OHIO

PEABODY MUSEUM OF ARCHAEOLOGY AND ETHNOLOGY, HARVARD UNIVERSITY,
CAMBRIDGE, MASSACHUSETTS

THE PICKER ART GALLERY, COLGATE UNIVERSITY, HAMILTON, NEW YORK

PRIVATE COLLECTION, CLEVELAND

PROPERTY FROM THE COLLECTION OF EDWARD AND NYMPHA MONTAGU

M. ULLOA COLLECTION

CHECKLIST OF THE EXHIBITION

TRANSFORMATION

1

*Standing figure wearing
helmet mask of killer whale*
West Mexico, Colima, Mexico
Preclassic–Classic, 200 B.C.–A.D. 400
solid ceramic
approx. 5 x 7.5 x 5 cm
National Museum of the American
Indian, Smithsonian Institution,New
York, New York, 23/693

2

*Figure with helmet mask and
face of animal on headdress*
Las Mercedes, Costa Rica
Period V–VI, A.D. 500–1200
greenstone
9.7 x 2.8 x 4 cm
National Museum of the American
Indian, Smithsonian Institution,
New York, New York, Exchange from
Dartmouth College Museum,
22/4535

Information in the checklist is presented
in the following order: descriptive title of
the object, culture, site or geographical
origin, excavator and date excavated
when known, name of period and dates,
medium, dimensions in centimeters in
the order height by width by depth,
museum, and collection information.

3

Face mask
West Mexico, Colima, Mexico
Preclassic–Classic, 200 B.C.–A.D. 400
burnished ceramic
22.8 x 17 x 5 cm
Birmingham Museum of Art, Birming-
ham, Alabama, Gift of Dr. and Mrs.
Charles W. Ochs, 1986.677

4

Face mask
West Mexico, Colima, Mexico
Preclassic–Classic, 200 B.C.–A.D. 400
burnished red ceramic
20.5 x 18.5 x 7 cm
Bowers Museum, Santa Ana, California

5

Dog with human face mask
West Mexico, Colima, Mexico
Preclassic–Classic, 200 B.C.–A.D. 400
burnished red ceramic
22.8 x 38.1 cm
Honolulu Academy of Arts, Honolulu,
Hawaii, 4173.1
Published in Oettinger 1985, p. 18,
fig. I-2

6

*Standing figure wearing
face mask*
West Mexico, Colima, Mexico
Preclassic–Classic, 200 B.C.–A.D. 400
red ceramic
26 x 11.5 x 16 cm
Private Collection, Cleveland

7

*Figure wearing jaguar helmet
mask, probably an incensario*
Classic Veracruz, Veracruz, Mexico
Classic, A.D. 600–900
gray ceramic, black asphalt paint,
incensario bowl broken from rear of
head
36.8 x 22.8 cm
Hudson Museum, University of
Maine, Orono, Maine, Palmer Collection, 197B

8

*Standing figure wearing
face mask and helmet, holding
figurine*
West Mexico, Colima, Mexico
Preclassic–Classic, 200 B.C.–A.D. 400
solid ceramic
19 x 10.8 x 8.2 cm
Hudson Museum, University of
Maine, Orono, Maine, Palmer
Collection, 354M

9

Nose and mouth ornament
Late Paracas-Early Nazca, South Coast
of Peru
Early Horizon-Early Intermediate, 400
B.C.–A.D. 200
gold
13.9 x 19 cm
The Cleveland Museum of Art, Cleveland, Ohio, Purchase from the J. H.
Wade Fund, 45.377

10

*Plaque of Oculate Being
with appendages*
Early Nazca, South Coast of Peru
Early Intermediate, 200 B.C.–A.D. 400
gold
18.4 x 21.5 cm
The Cleveland Museum of Art, Cleveland, Ohio, Gift of the Hanna Fund,
57.26

11

Gold pectoral of feline face
Tolita, Ecuador
Regional Developmental, 500
B.C.–A.D.500
gold
12.7 x 30.4 x 4.4 cm
Collection of Mr. and Mrs. Luis
Naboa, New York
Published in Stierlin 1984, p. 103, no.
87

12

*Figure with saurian–feline face,
clawed hands and feet*
Jama Coaque, San Isidro, Manabí,
Ecuador
Regional Developmental, 500
B.C.–A.D. 500
ceramic, buff and blue paint
27.9 x 19.6 x 20.3 cm
Museo Antropológico, Banco Central
de Ecuador, Guayaquil, Ecuador, GA-
1-1855-81

13

*Standing figure in avian
(parrot) costume*
Jama Coaque, Ecuador
Regional Developmental, 500
B.C.–A.D. 500
ceramic
17.5 x 10.5 cm
Museo Antropológico, Banco Central
de Ecuador, Guayaquil, Ecuador,
GA–35–614–78

14

Face mask
Olmec, Mexico
Preclassic, 900–600 B.C.
serpentine
10.8 x 8.2 x 3.1 cm
Hudson Museum, University of
Maine, Orono, Maine, Palmer Collection, 207M

15

Face mask
Olmec, Central Mexico
Preclassic, 1150–900 B.C.
gray ceramic
17.7 x 15.8 cm
Krannert Art Museum and Kinkead
Pavilion, University of Illinois at Champaign-Urbana, Illinois, Collection of
Mr. Fred Schmidt, Promised gift to
the Krannert Art Museum

16

"Ai Aipec" Mask
Moche, North Coast, Peru
Early Intermediate, 200 B.C.–A.D. 600
17 x 23.2 cm
copper with shell inlay
Museo Arqueológico Rafael Larco Herrera, Lima, Peru

17

*Figurine of shaman with
Olmec face mask*
Tlapacoya, Mexico
Preclassic, 1150–550 B.C.
solid ceramic
17 x 7.5 x 9.5 cm

National Museum of the American
Indian, Smithsonian Institution,
New York, New York, 24/2726

18

*Pectoral of feline face for
kuraka's dance costume*
Trujillo Region, North Coast, Peru
Colonial, 17th–18th Century
gold, repoussé
25 x 33 x 3.1 cm
Krannert Art Museum and Kinkead
Pavilion at University of Illinois at
Champaign-Urbana, Illinois,
Purchase and Gift of Mr. Fred Olsen,
67-29-521

PORTRAITURE

19

Face mask
Olmec, Rió Pesquero, Veracruz, Mexico
Preclassic, 900–600 B.C.
jade, burnt
17.1 x 15.2 cm
Honolulu Academy of Arts, Honolulu,
Hawaii

20

*Face mask with geometric
designs*
Chupícuaro, Guanajuato, Mexico
Late Preclassic, 500–100 B.C.
ceramic, paint
19.3 x 17.4 x 2.5 cm
National Museum of the American
Indian, Smithsonian Institution,
New York, New York, 24/6500

21

Miniature mask
Mixtec, Puebla, Mexico
Postclassic, A.D. 1200–1500
ceramic with blue, red, and white
paint
9 x 9.5 x 5 cm
National Museum of the American
Indian, Smithsonian Institution,
New York, New York, 18/5880

22
*Mask with holes for inlays
in eyes*
Teotihuacán, Mexico
Middle Classic, A.D. 300–750
greenstone
16.5 x 16.5 x 7.6 cm
Birmingham Museum of Art, Birmingham, Alabama, Gift of Gay Barna in
memory of her mother, Rose Mont-
gomery Melhado, AFI 25.1982

23
*Miniature mask with incised
facial decorations*
Jama Coaque, Miguelillo, Manabí,
Ecuador
Regional Developmental, 500
B.C.–A.D. 500
ceramic
10 x 9.5 cm
Museo Antropológico, Banco Central
de Ecuador, Guayaquil, Ecuador, GA-
2-2499-83

24
*Miniature mask with raised
designs*
Jama Coaque, Pedernales, Ecuador
Regional Developmental, 500
B.C.–A.D. 500
ceramic, buff and blue paint
8.8 x 10.1 cm
Museo Antropológico, Banco Central
de Ecuador, Guayaquil, Ecuador, GA-
4-2231-82

25
*Figure wearing headdress with
bird and central mask, holding
rattle and panpipes*
Jama Coaque, Ecuador
Regional Developmental, 500
B.C.–A.D. 500
ceramic, black paint
27.3 x 15.2 x 27.9 cm
Museo Antropológico, Banco Central
de Ecuador, Guayaquil, Ecuador, GA-
2-1079-78

26
Face mask of old man
Classic Veracruz, Veracruz, Mexico
Classic, A.D. 600–900
ceramic, traces of paint
17.1 x 16.5 x 6.3 cm
Property from the Collection of
Edward and Nympha Montagu,
Buffalo, New York

27
Face mask of old man
Virú Culture, North Coast, Peru
Early Intermediate, ca. 250 B.C.
ceramic, painted with bitumen on
brow and chin
20.3 x 20 x 8.4 cm
Krannert Art Museum and Kinkead
Pavilion, University of Illinois at
Champaign-Urbana, Illinois, Purchase
and Gift of Mr. Fred Olsen, 67-29-196
Published in Sawyer 1975, p. 23, fig.
25

28
*Face mask with headdress with
half–moon, feline decorations,
and circular earrings*
Moche, North Coast, Peru
Early Intermediate, 200 B.C.–A.D. 600
ceramic
18.9 x 18.1 cm
Museo Nacional de Arqueología y
Antropología, Lima, Peru, CO2398

29
*Face mask with knotted head-
dress with feline ornament*
Moche, North Coast, Peru
Early Intermediate, 200 B.C.–A.D. 600
ceramic
19.5 x 16.5 cm
Museo Nacional de Arqueología y
Antropología, Lima, Peru, CO2395

30
*Face mask with lower half
painted red*
Michoacán, Mexico
Postclassic, A.D. 1200–1500

ceramic, paint, copper
15.4 x 14.5 x 4 cm
National Museum of the American
Indian, Smithsonian Institution,
New York, New York, 23/6927

31
Pectoral with feline face
Macaracas, Sitio Conte, Panama,
excavated by S.K. Lothrop
Period V–VI, A.D. 500–1100
gold
9.5 x 10 cm
The Cleveland Museum of Art, Cleve-
land, Ohio, Thirty-Fifth Anniversary
Gift, The Norweb Collection, 51.155
Published in Lothrop 1937–42, part 1,
p. 285, fig. 252

32
*Mask with serrated crest and
painted designs*
Playa Venado, Panama, excavated by
Neville A. Hart
Period V, A.D. 500–1000
ceramic, paint
25.5 x 24 x 13 cm
Peabody Museum of Archaeology and
Ethnology, Harvard University, Cam-
bridge, Massachusetts, 51-35-20/
18511

BURIAL AND
SUBSTITUTION

33
Mask, holes for inlays in eyes
Teotihuacán, Mexico
Middle Classic, A.D. 300–750
serpentine
13.3 x 11.2 cm
The Baltimore Museum of Art, Balti-
more, Maryland, Gift of Edith Black,
Potomac, Maryland, in memory of
her husband Jack Black, 1984.233

34
Face mask
Hidalgo, Mexico
Postclassic, A.D. 1000–1200
stone
15.2 x 12.6 x 9 cm
American Museum of Natural History,
New York, New York, 30/11817

35
False head for mortuary bundle
Pachacamac, Peru
Middle Horizon–Late Intermediate,
A.D. 800–1200
wood with shell inlays, textiles, feathers
27 x 19 cm
American Museum of Natural History,
New York, New York, collected by
Adolph Bandelier, B/7737

36
False head for mortuary bundle
Huari, Central Coast, Peru
Middle Horizon, A.D. 600–1000
textiles, feathers, reeds
38.1 x 25.4 x 17.7 cm
Collection of Arthur G. Rosen, New
Jersey

37
*Face for false head for mortuary
bundle*
Huara, Central Coast, Peru
Middle Horizon, A.D. 700–1000
wood with traces of paint
50.1 x 18 x 9.8 cm
Krannert Art Museum and Kinkead
Pavilion, University of Illinois at Cham-
paign-Urbana, Illinois, Purchase and
Gift of Mr. Fred Olsen, 67–29–300

38
*Face for false head for mortuary
bundle*
Huara, Central Coast, Peru
Middle Horizon, A.D. 700–1000
wood, plaster, red and black paint;

made in three pieces
25.4 x 25.4 x 8.8 cm
Krannert Art Museum and Kinkead
Pavilion at University of Illinois at
Champaign–Urbana, Illinois, Purchase
and Gift of Mr. Fred Olsen,
67–29–344
Published in Sawyer 1975, p. 128, fig.
190

39
Mask
Sicán, North Coast, Peru
Late Intermediate, Middle Sicán,
A.D. 850–1050
gold
23.5 x 51 cm
Museo Arqueológico Regional Brun-
ing, Lambayeque, Peru

40
Mask
Sicán, North Coast, Peru
Late Intermediate, Middle Sicán,
A.D. 850–1050
gold
19.5 x 32.2 cm
Museo Arqueológico Regional Brun-
ing, Lambayeque, Peru

41
False head for mortuary bundle
(not exhibited)
El Castillo, Huacho, Peru
Middle Horizon, A.D. 800–1000
wooden mask with red, white, and
black paint; cotton textiles, silver
headband, and four metal pins;
stuffed with leaves
53 x 53 x 11 cm
Peabody Museum of Archaeology and
Ethnology, Harvard University,
Cambridge, Massachusetts, 30/3541
Published in Bawden and
Conrad 1982, p. 81

42
*Face mask with geometric
decoration and parallel lines
crossing the face*
Chancay, Central Coast, Peru

Late Intermediate, A.D. 1100–1400
ceramic, white with red and black
paint, fabric ties in suspension holes
18 x 15.5 cm
Museo Amano, Miraflores, Peru,
R.00.95

43
Face mask
Late Intrusive Woodlands, Heinish
Mound, Scioto County, Ohio
Woodlands, 1000 B.C.–A.D. 500
stone
15 x 11 x 8 cm
Ohio Historical Society, Columbus,
Ohio

44
Face mask
Peña Blanca, near Chilanga, Morazan,
El Salvador
steatite
18 x 18 x 3.5 cm
National Museum of the American
Indian, Smithsonian Institution, New
York, New York, collected by S. K.
Lothrop, 13/601

STATE-LEVEL SOCIETIES

45
Face mask
Aztec, Valley of Mexico
Postclassic, A.D. 1300–1521
ceramic
18.4 cm
American Museum of Natural History,
New York, New York, 30/504

46
Mask of the Merchant God
Huastec, Veracruz, Mexico
Postclassic, A.D. 1200–1500
gray ceramic, black paint
12.7 x 11.4 x 6.3 cm
Hudson Museum, University of
Maine, Orono, Maine, Palmer
Collection, 351M

47
Miniature mask
Olmec, Mexico
Preclassic, 900–600 B.C.
stone
5.7 x 4.4 x 1.9 cm
Mexican Museum, San Francisco,
California, 1981.18.1

48
Mask of Were–jaguar
Olmec, Mexico
Preclassic, 900–600 B.C.
stone
14.6 x 12 x 6.3 cm
Mexican Museum, San Francisco, California, 1981.6

49
Face with double–headed fire serpent headdress
Mixtec, Oaxaca or Puebla, Mexico
Postclassic, A.D. 1200–1500
serpentine
8.8 x 5 x 7.6 cm
The Baltimore Museum of Art, Baltimore, Maryland, Gift of Alan Wurtzburger, 1960.30.31
Published in Kubler 1958, p. 22, no. 25

50
Incensario maskette
Teotihuacán, Mexico
Middle Classic, A.D. 300–750
ceramic, red, yellow, and black paint
11.4 x 13.5 x 6.3 cm
Hudson Museum, University of Maine, Orono, Maine, Palmer Collection, 69A34

51
Head
Teotihuacán, Mexico
Middle Classic, A.D. 300–750
translucent green onyx marble (*tecali*)
broken from a figure
14.6 x 12 x 5 cm

Collection of Harry and Maxula Mannil, Caracas, Venezuela, MAN-A

52
Face mask
Teotihuacán, Mexico
Middle Classic, A.D. 300–750
greenstone
19 x 16.5 x 5 cm
Hudson Museum, University of Maine, Orono, Maine, Palmer Collection, 290M

53
Mold-made mask with glyph on forehead
Maya, Jaina style, Guaymil, Campeche, Mexico
Late Classic, A.D. 550–950
ceramic, paint
15.5 x 12.6 x 6.5 cm
National Museum of the American Indian, Smithsonian Institution, New York, New York, 24/496

54
Mask
Maya, Cenote of Sacrifice, Chichén Itzá, Mexico
Early Postclassic, A.D. 900–1100
sheet gold, hammered, cut and embossed
8.7 x 7.5 cm
Peabody Museum of Archaeology and Ethnology, Harvard University, Cambridge, Massachusetts, 10–71–20/C–7689B
Published in Lothrop 1952, p. 64, fig. 48b; Willard 1941, facing p. 93; Coggins and Shane 1984, p. 96

55
Mosaic face mask
Mixtec, Acatlan, Puebla, Mexico
Postclassic, A.D. 1200–1500
wood, paint, stone tesserae
16.5 x 13.7 x 7 cm
National Museum of the American Indian, Smithsonian Institution, New York, New York, collected by C. A. Purpus 10/8714

Published in Saville 1922, p. 45, pl. xiv

56
Face mask with holes for inlays in eyes
Tres Zapotes, Veracruz, Mexico
Preclassic, 100 B.C.–A.D. 300
serpentine
12 x 5 x 10 cm
The Baltimore Museum of Art, Baltimore, Maryland, Gift of Alan Wurtzburger, 1960.30.25
Published in Kubler 1958, p. 24, no. 31

57
Face mask
Mixtec, Oaxaca or Puebla, Mexico
Postclassic, A.D. 1200–1500
greenstone
12.7 x 10.1 x 6.3 cm
Hudson Museum, University of Maine, Orono, Maine, Palmer Collection, 138M

58
Face mask
Mexico
Postclassic, A.D. 1200–1500
gray stone
17 x 15 x 8.2 cm
Houston Museum of Fine Arts, Houston, Texas, 87.77

ARCHITECTURE

59
Statue of Xipe Totec
Huastec or Aztec, Veracruz, Mexico
Postclassic, A.D. 1200–1500
ceramic
133.9 x 39.3 x 35.5 cm

Hudson Museum, University of Maine, Orono, Maine, Palmer Collection, 305M

60

Statue of Ehecatl, God of the Wind
Veracruz, Mexico
Postclassic, A.D. 900–1500
ceramic
78 x 40 x 24 cm
Hudson Museum, University of Maine, Orono, Maine, Palmer Collection, 544M

61

Hollow crested human head with suspension holes
Classic Veracruz, Pyramid of the Niches, El Tajín, Veracruz, Mexico
Classic, A.D. 600–900
scoria
23.5 x 14 x 15.5 cm
National Museum of the American Indian, Smithsonian Institution, New York, New York, 20/1841

62

Mask with holes for inlays and suspension
Teotihuacán style, found in Tlatelolco, Mexico
Middle Classic, A.D. 300–750
greenstone
27 x 31.5 x 15 cm
National Museum of the American Indian, Smithsonian Institution, New York, New York, ex–Conde de Penasco collection, 2/6607
Published in Mayer [1843], p. 274

63

Mask with fanged mouth
Central Mexico
Colonial, 16th–18th Century
stone with traces of red and green stucco
25.5 x 23 x 13 cm
National Museum of the American Indian, Smithsonian Institution, New York, New York
[CAT. NO. 63]

25.5 x 23 x 13 cm
National Museum of the American Indian, Smithsonian Institution, New York, New York, 15/5596

64

Mask
Mixtec, Oaxaca or Puebla, Mexico
Postclassic, A.D. 1200–1500
gray stone
15.5 x 14 cm
Honolulu Academy of Arts, Honolulu, Hawaii, 4154.1

65

Face mask
Belize, Harrison, Belize
greenstone
18 x 18 x 3.5 cm
National Museum of the American Indian, Smithsonian Institution, New York, New York, Thomas Gann Collection 9/6396

66

Mask
Tarascan, Santa Fe la Laguna, Michoacán, Mexico
Postclassic, A.D. 1200–1530
scoria
31.5 x 28 x 8.2 cm
National Museum of the American Indian, Smithsonian Institution, New York, New York, Exchange with Julius Carlebach, 17/6162

67

Standing figure holding vessel and foliage, wearing mask backpiece
Izapan style, reportedly from Colima
Preclassic–Classic, 200 B.C.–A.D. 400
burnished red ceramic
47.6 x 28.5 x 22.8 cm
Hudson Museum, University of Maine, Orono, Maine, Palmer Collection, 307M

68

Mask
Sicán, North Coast, Peru
Late Intermediate, Middle Sicán, A.D.

850–1050
gold
26 x 47.6 x 7.6 cm
M. Ulloa Collection

69

Miniature mask
Chontal, Guerrero, Mexico
Classic–Postclassic
alabaster
8.2 x 5.7 x 3.8 cm
The Picker Art Gallery, Colgate University, Hamilton, New York

RITUAL PERFORMANCE

70

Tlaloc-masked ballplayer
San Miguel, Atzcapotzalco, Mexico
Preclassic
solid ceramic
9.2 x 7 x 3.5 cm
National Museum of the American Indian, Smithsonian Institution, New York, New York, H. H. Rice Collection 9/3010

71

Elliptical miniature mask
Taino, Puerto Rico
Period IV, A.D. 1000–1500
stone
14 x 11 x 4 cm
National Museum of the American Indian, Smithsonian Institution, New York, New York, ex–Felix Seijo Collection, 3/1986

72

Rectangular face mask
Tierradentro, Colombia
Tierradentro, date undetermined
painted ceramic
20.7 x 15.2 x 5.4 cm
Dr. Stephen Blair, Newport Beach, California

73

Face mask with four phallic figures on headdress

Nariño, Colombia
Late period, Tuza Ceramic Complex, A.D. 1250–1500
ceramic with paint
32 x 17.7 x 4.5 cm
Dr. Stephen Blair, Newport Beach, California

74

Cast of wooden face mask

Calusa, Key Marco, Florida. Original excavated by Frank Hamilton Cushing, 1895–96
Late Mississippian, A.D. 1400–1500
plaster copy of original wood, with paint
23.5 x 14 x 7 cm
Mrs. Marion Gilliland, Gainesville, Florida
Original published in Gilliland 1989, p. 90 and 98, pls. 43 and 51

75

Cast of wooden face mask

Calusa, Key Marco, Florida. Original excavated by Frank Hamilton Cushing, 1895–96
Late Mississippian, A.D. 1400–1500
plaster copy of original wood, with paint, shell inlays in eyes
26 x 14 x 8.5 cm
Mrs. Marion Gilliland, Gainesville, Florida
Original published in Gilliland, 1989, p. 104, pl. 57

76

Face mask with serpent design on side of face

West Mexico, Colima, Mexico
Preclassic–Classic, 200 B.C.–A.D. 400
spondylus shell
12.5 x 12.4 x 2.5 cm

National Museum of the American Indian, Smithsonian Institution, New York, New York, 24/8701

77

Long-Nosed-God miniature mask

Green County, Kentucky
Mississippian, A.D. 1200–1500
shell
3.5 x 1.8 x 1.9 cm
National Museum of the American Indian, Smithsonian Institution, New York, New York, Collection of Bennett H. Young, 4/7878

78

Shell gorget of human face painted red

Cross County, Arkansas
Mississippian, A.D. 1200–1500
shell with red paint
11.5 x 10 x 2.3 cm
National Museum of the American Indian, Smithsonian Institution, New York, New York, Loan from the Academy of Natural Sciences of Philadelphia, 16/7671

79

Rectangular face mask with eyes pierced through

Cementerio de Quibor, Venezuela
Late, A.D. 300–1000
ceramic
13.3 x 15.2 x 2.5 cm
Collection of Harry and Maxula Mannil, Caracas, Venezuela, MAN-U9
Published in Arroyo C. et al. 1971, p. 142, no. 209

80

Face mask

Vicús, Piura Region, North Peru
A.D. 100–800
ceramic, with white painted stripes

29 x 30 cm
Museo Arqueológico Rafael Larco Herrera, Lima, Peru

81 A–G

Seven miniature helmet masks

Nopiloa, Classic Veracruz, Veracruz, Mexico
Classic, A.D. 600–900
ceramic with black asphalt paint
A. 23/3513 8 x 6.5 x 6.5 cm;
B. 23/3514 6.5 x 6.7 x 6.5 cm;
C. 23/3515 7 x 7.2 x 6.6 cm;
D. 23/3516 7 x 6.3 x 8 cm;
E. 23/3517 8 x 7.1 x 10.5 cm;
F. 23/3518 7.3 x 6 x 6.5 cm;
G. 23/3519 9.8 x 6.5 x 7 cm
National Museum of the American Indian, Smithsonian Institution, New York, New York, 23/3513–3519

82

Standing figure with saurian face on headdress holding rattles

Jama Coaque, Ecuador
Regional Developmental, 500 B.C.–A.D. 500
ceramic
36.8 x 22.2 x 13.9 cm
Museo Antropológico, Banco Central de Ecuador, Guayaquil, Ecuador, GA–1–2179–82

83

Head with coil–patterned mask, projecting eyes and mouth

Jama Coaque, Ecuador
Regional Developmental, 500 B.C.–A.D. 500
ceramic; broken from a figure
13.6 x 10 x 9.5 cm
Museo Antropológico, Banco Central de Ecuador, Guayaquil, Ecuador, GA-18–1677-80

BIBLIOGRAPHY

Alva, Walter. "New Tomb of Royal Splendor: The Moche of Ancient Peru," *National Geographic*, vol. 177, no. 6, 1990, pp. 2-16.

Arroyo C., Miguel, J. M. Cruxent, and Sagrario Perez Soto de Atencio. *Arte Prehispánico de Venezuela*. Caracas, Fundación Eugenio Mendoza, 1971.

Bawden, Garth, and Geoffrey W. Conrad. *The Andean Heritage*. Cambridge, Peabody Museum Press, 1982.

Benson, Elizabeth P. *The Olmec and Their Neighbors, Essays in Memory of Matthew W. Stirling*. Washington D.C., Dumbarton Oaks, 1981.

Berlo, Janet Catherine. "Artistic Specialization at Teotihuacán: The Ceramic Incense Burner," in Alana Cordy-Collins (ed.), *Pre-Columbian Art History: Selected Readings* [2nd. ed.]. Palo Alto, California, Peek Publications, 1982, pp. 83-100.

Borgatti, Jean M., and Richard Brilliant. *Likeness and Beyond: Portraits from Africa and the World*. New York, The Center for African Art, 1990.

Broda, Johanna. "El tributo en trajes guerreros y la estructura del sistema tributaria Mexica," in Pedro Carrasco and Johanna Broda (eds.), *Economía, política e ideología en el México Prehispánico*, pp. 115-174. INAH, Mexico, 1978.

Broda, Johanna. "Tlacaxipehualiztli: A Reconstruction of an Aztec Calendar Festival from Sixteenth Century Sources," *Revista Española de Antropología Americana*, vol. 6, pp. 245-327. Madrid, 1970.

Brose, David S., James A. Brown, and David W. Penny. *Ancient Art of the American Woodland Indians*. New York, Harry N. Abrams and the Detroit Institute of Art, 1985.

Brunius, Teddy. "The Uses of Masks in Different Cultures, Particularly Death Masks," in Beatríz de la Fuente and Louise Noelle (eds.), *Arte funerario* (Coloquio Internacional de Historia del Arte), vol. 1, pp. 273-277. Mexico, U.N.A.M., 1987.

Burgos, Julio. *Mascaras Precolumbinas en la costa Ecuatoriana*. Guayaquil, Museo Antropológico del Banco Central del Ecuador, 1981.

Carmichael, Elizabeth M. *Turquoise Mosaics from Mexico*. London, British Museum, 1970.

Caso, Alfonso. *Reyes y reinos de la Mixteca*. 2 vols. Mexico, Fondo de Cultura Económica, 1977-79.

Coe, Michael D. *The Jaguar's Children: Preclassic Central Mexico*. New York, The Museum of Primitive Art, 1965

Coe, Michael D. *America's First Civilization*. New York, American Heritage, 1968.

Coggins, Clemency Chase, and Orrin C. Shane III (eds.). *Cenote of Sacrifice: Maya Treasures from the Sacred Wall at Chichén Itzá*. Austin, Science Museum of Minnesota, 1984.

Cole, Herbert M. (ed.). *I Am Not Myself: The Art of African Masquerade*, Monograph Series no. 26. Los Angeles, Museum of Cultural History, UCLA, 1985.

Cook, Richard G., and Warwick Bray. "The Goldwork of Panama: An Iconographic and Chronological Perspective," in Jones, 1985, pp. 34-35.

Corona Nuñez, José. *Antigüedades de México, basadas en la recopilación de Lord Kingsborough*. 4 vols. Mexico, Secretaria de Hacienda y Credito, 1964–67.

Couch, N. C. Christopher. *Pre-Columbian Art from the Ernest Erickson Collection at the American Museum of Natural History*. New York, American Museum of Natural History, 1988.

Couch, N. C. Christopher. "A Comparison of Helmet Mask Figures from Three Pacific Coastal Areas," in *Proceedings, Sociedad Mexicana de antropología, XVII Mesa Redonda*. Mexico, in press.

Craine, Eugene R., and Reginald C. Reindorp (eds. and trans.). *The Chroni-*

cles of Michoacán. Norman, University of Oklahoma Press, 1970.

Cummins, Tom. "We Are the Other: Peruvian Portraits of Colonial Kurakas," in Rolena Adorno and Kenneth J. Andrein, *Trans-Atlantic Encounters: Europeans and Andeans in the Sixteenth Century.* London, Berkeley, and Los Angeles, University of California Press, in press.

Dawson, Larry in Ann Pollard Rowe, Elizabeth P. Benson, and Anne-Louise Schaffer (eds.), *The Junius B. Bird Pre-Columbian Textile Conference, May 19th and 20th, 1973.* Washington, D.C., The Textile Museum and Dumbarton Oaks, 1979.

Delgado R., Lelia, and Luis E. Molina. *Arte Prehispánico del Valle de Quibor, habitantes de lo imaginario.* Caracas, Galería de Arte Nacional, 1983.

Dockstader, Frederick. *Indian Art in Middle America.* Greenwich, Connecticut, New York Graphic Society, 1964.

Durán, Diego. *Historía de las Indias de Nueva España.* 2 vols. Angel Maria Garibay K. (ed.). Mexico, Editorial Porrua, 1967.

Dwyer, Jane Powell. "The Chronology and Iconography of Paracas-Style Textiles," in Ann Pollard Rowe, Elizabeth P. Benson, and Anne-Louise Schaffer (eds.), *The Junius B. Bird Pre-Columbian Textile Conference, May 19th and 20th, 1973,* pp. 105-128. Washington D.C., The Textile Museum and Dumbarton Oaks, 1979.

Dwyer, Jane Powell. "The Paracas Cemeteries: Mortuary Patterns in a Peruvian South Coastal Tradition," in Elizabeth P. Benson (ed.), *Death and the Afterlife in Pre-Columbian America,* pp. 145-161. Dumbarton Oaks, Washington D.C., 1975.

Ekholm, Gordon. "Puerto Rican Stone 'Collars' as Ballgame Belts," in Samuel K. Lothrop et al., *Essays in Pre-Columbian Art and Archaeology,* pp. 356–371. Cambridge, Harvard University Press, 1961.

Fewkes, J. Walter. "Puerto Rican Elbow Stones in the Heye Museum with Discussion of Similar Objects Elsewhere," *American Anthropologist,* vol. 15, no. 3, 1913, pp. 435-459.

Fleming, S. J., W. C. Miller, and J. L. Brahin. "The Mummies of Pachacamac, Peru," *MASCA Journal,* vol. 2, no. 5, 1983, pp. 138-156. Philadelphia, Museum of Applied Science, Center for Archaeology, University Museum, University of Pennsylvania, 1983.

Furst, Jill Leslie, and Peter T. Furst. *Pre-Columbian Art of Mexico.* New York, Abbeville Press, 1980.

Furst, Peter T. "West Mexican Tomb Sculptures as Evidence for Shamanism," *Antropológica,* no. 16, (Dic.) 1965. (Caracas).

Gilliland, Marion Spjut. "Marco's Buried Treasure: Wetlands Archaeology and Adventure in Nineteenth Century Florida," in Barbara A. Purdy (ed.), *Wet Site Archaeology,* pp. 255–261. Caldwell, New Jersey, The Telford Press, 1988.

Gilliland, Marion Spjut. *The Material Culture of Key Marco, Florida.* Gainesville, Florida Classics Library, 1989.

Griffin, Gillette C. "Olmec Forms and Materials Found in Central Guerrero," in Benson, 1981, pp. 209–222.

Grove, David C. *The Olmec Paintings of Oxtotitlán Cave, Guerrero, Mexico.* Studies in Pre-Columbian Art and Archaeology, no. 6. Washington, D.C., Dumbarton Oaks, 1970.

Hainaux, René. "Editorial," *World Theater,* vol. 10, no. 1, 1961, pp. 3–10.

Hammer, Olga. *Ancient Art of Veracruz.* Los Angeles, Ethnic Arts Council of Los Angeles, 1971.

Heyden, Doris, and Paul Gendrop. *Pre-Columbian Architecture of Mesoamerica.* New York, Harry N. Abrams, 1973.

Jones, Julie (ed.). *The Art of Pre-Columbian Gold: The Jan Mitchell Collection.* Boston, Little, Brown, and Company, 1985.

Joralemon, Peter David. *A Study of Olmec Iconography.* Studies in Pre-Columbian Art and Architecture, no.

7. Washington, D.C., Dumbarton Oaks, 1971.

Joralemon, Peter David. "The Olmec Dragon: A Study in Pre-Columbian Iconography," in H. B. Nicholson (ed.), *Origins of Religious Art and Iconography in Preclassic Mesoamerica,* pp. 27-72. UCLA Latin American Studies Series, vol. 31. Los Angeles, UCLA Latin American Center Publications and Ethnic Arts Council of Los Angeles, 1976.

Klein, Cecelia F. "Masking Empire: The Material Effects of Masks in Aztec Mexico," *Art History,* vol. 9, no. 2, 1986.

Klein, Cecelia F. "Tlaloc Masks as Insignia of Office in the Mexica-Aztec Hierarchy," in Janet Brody Esser (ed.), *Behind the Mask in Mexico,* pp. 6–27. Santa Fe, Museum of International Folk Art, 1988.

Kubler, George. "Notes on the Collection," in *The Alan Wutzburger Collection of Pre-Columbian Art,* pp. 14–40. Baltimore, The Baltimore Museum of Art, 1958.

Kubler, George. *The Art and Architecture of Ancient America: The Mexican, Maya, and Andean Peoples.* 3d. ed. Harmondsworth, Penguin Books, 1984.

Labbé, Armand J. *Colombia before Columbus.* New York, Rizzoli, 1986.

Levi-Strauss, Claude. *The Way of the Masks.* Sylvia Modelski (trans.). Seattle, University of Washington Press, 1982.

Lothrop, Samuel K. *Coclé: An Archaeological Study of Central Panama. Pts. 1 and 2.* Memoirs of the Peabody Museum of Archaeology and Ethnology, vols. 7 and 8, Harvard University, Cambridge, 1937–1942.

Lothrop, Samuel K. *Metals from the Cenote of Sacrifice, Chichén Itzá, Yucatán.* Memoirs of the Peabody Museum of Archaeology and Ethnology, vol. 10, no. 2., Harvard University, Cambridge, 1952.

Lothrop, Samuel K. "The Museum Central American Expedition," 1925-26, *Indian Notes,* vol. 4, no. 1, p.12–33.

Markman, Roberta H., and Peter T. Markman. *Masks of the Spirit*. Berkeley and Los Angeles, University of California Press, 1989.

Mayer, Brantz. *Mexico As It Was and As It Is*. New York, J. Winchester, New World Press [1843].

Meggers, Betty J. *Ecuador*. New York, Praeger, 1966.

Mexico: Splendors of Thirty Centuries. New York, The Metropolitan Museum of Art, 1990.

Milbrath, Susan. *A Study of Olmec Sculptural Chronology*. Studies in Pre-Columbian Art and Archaeology no. 23. Washington, D.C., Dumbarton Oaks, 1979.

Miller, Mary Ellen. *The Murals of Bonampak*. Princeton, Princeton University Press, 1986.

Mills, William C. "Exploration of the Mound City Group," in *Ohio Archaeological and Historical Publications*, vol. 31, pp. 423–585, 1922.

Moser, Christopher L. "A Postclassic Burial Cave in the Southern Cañada," in Kent Flannery and Joyce Marcus (eds.), *The Cloud People*. New York, Academic Press, 1983.

Napier, A. David. *Masks, Transformation, and Paradox*. Berkeley, Los Angeles, and London, University of California Press, 1986.

Natalie Wood Collection of Pre-Columbian Ceramics from Chupícuaro, Guanajuato, Mexico at U.C.L.A. Los Angeles, Museum and Laboratory of Ethnic Arts and Technology, University of California, 1969.

Oettinger, Marion. *Dancing Faces, Mexican Masks in a Cultural Context*. Washington D.C., Meridian House International, 1985.

Parsons, Lee A., John B. Carlson, and Peter David Joralemon. *The Face of Ancient America: The Wally and Brenda Zollman Collection of Pre-Columbian Art*. Indianapolis, Indianapolis Museum of Art and Indiana University Press, 1988.Pasztory, Esther. *Aztec Art*. New York, Harry N. Abrams, 1983.

Pasztory, Esther. "Texts, Archaeology, Art, and History in Templo Mayor: Reflections," in Elizabeth Boone (ed.), *In the Aztec Templo Mayor; A Symposium at Dumbarton Oaks, 8th and 9th October 1983*, pp. 451–462, Washington, D.C., Dumbarton Oaks, 1987.

Pasztory, Esther. *Aztec Art*. New York, Harry N. Abrams, 1983

Pasztory, Esther. "A Reinterpretation of Teotihuacán and its Mural Painting Tradition," in Kathleen Berrin (ed.), *Feathered Serpents and Flowering Trees*, pp. 45–77. San Francisco, Fine Arts Museum of San Francisco, 1988.

Paul, Anne. *Paracas*. Norman, University of Oklahoma Press, 1990.

Paul, Anne, and Solveig A. Turpin. "The Ecstatic Shaman Theme of Paracas Textiles," *Archaeology*, vol. 39, 1986, pp. 20-27.

Pernet, Henry. "Masks, Theoretical Perspectives, Ritual Masks in Nonliterature Cultures," in Mircea Eliade (ed.), *The Encyclopedia of Religion*, vol. 9, pp. 259–269. New York and London, Collier Macmillan, 1987.

Peterson, Jeanette Favrot. *Pre-Columbian Flora and Fauna*. San Diego, Mingei International Museum of World Folk Art, 1990.

Price, Sally. *Primitive Art in Civilized Places*. Chicago, The University of Chicago Press, 1989.

Proskouriakoff, Tatiana. "Classic Art of Central Veracruz," in Robert Wauchope (ed.), *Handbook of Middle American Indians*, vol. 11, pp. 558–572. Austin, University of Texas Press, 1971.

Proulx, Donald. "Headhunting in Ancient Peru," *Archaeology*, vol. 24, no. 1, 1971, pp. 16–21.

Robertson, Merle Green. *The Sculptures of Palenque*. Vols. 1-3. Princeton, Princeton University Press, 1983–1987

Saville, Marshall H. *Turquoise Mosaic Art in Ancient Mexico*. Contributions from the Museum of the American Indian, Heye Foundation, vol. 6. New York, Museum of the American Indian, 1922.

Sawyer, Alan R. *Ancient Andean Art in the Collection of the Krannert Art Museum*. Urbana-Champaign, Illinois, Krannert Art Museum, 1975.

Scott, John F. "The Role of Mesoamerican Funerary Figures," in Beatríz de la Fuente and Louise Noelle (eds.), *Arte funerario* (Coloquio Internacional de historía del arte), vol. 2, pp. 7–16. Mexico, U.N.A.M., 1987.

Shimada, Izumi, and Paloma Carcedo Muro. "Behind the Golden Mask: The Sicán Gold Artifacts from Batán Grande, Peru," in Jones, 1985, pp. 60–75.

Stierlin, Henri. *Art of the Incas*. New York, Rizzoli, 1984.

Stone, Doris. *Pre-Columbian Man Finds Central America, the Archaeological Bridge*. Cambridge, Harvard University Press, 1972.

Umberger, Emily Good. *Aztec Sculptures, Hieroglyphs, and History*. Doctoral dissertation, Department of Art History, Columbia University. Ann Arbor, University Microfilms, 1981.

Weaver, Muriel Noe Porter. "Excavations at Chupícuaro, Guanajuato, Mexico," *American Philosophical Society, Transactions*, vol. 46, no. 5, pp. 515–637, Philadelphia, 1956.

Weigand, Phil C. "Evidence for Complex Societies During the Western Mesoamerican Classic Period," in Michael C. Foster and Phil C. Weigand (eds.), *The Archaeology of West and Northwest Mesoamerica*. Boulder, Westview Press, 1985.

Willard, Theodore Arthur. *Kukulcan the Bearded Conqueror: New Mayan Discoveries*. Hollywood, California, Murray and Gee, 1941.

Willey, Gordon R. *Introduction to American Archaeology*, vol. 2, South America. Englewood Cliffs, New Jersey, Prentice-Hall, 1971.

Winning, Hasso von. *The Shaft Tomb Figures of West Mexico*. Southwest Museum Papers, no. 24. Los Angeles, Southwest Museum, 1974.

THE EXHIBITION

Curator
N. C. Christopher Couch

Coordinator
Allen Wardwell

*Director of Visual Arts Program,
Americas Society*
Fatima Bercht

*Production Coordinator
and Registrar*
Randolph Black

Tour Coordinator
Barbara Berger

Exhibition Designer
Michael Rizzo

Editor
Jacquelyn Hamm Southern

Conservation Consultant
Ellen Pearlstein

Mount Makers
David Horack
Elaine Manne

Curatorial Assistant
Gwen Allen

Registrarial Assistant
Lisa Leavitt

Art Handlers
Michael Bundy
Canon Hudson

Coordinators in Peru
Binomio

THE CATALOGUE

Author
N. C. Christopher Couch

Editors
Joanna Eckman
Daniel Jussim
Jacquelyn Hamm Southern

Production Coordinator
Barbara Berger

Research Assistant
Gwen Allen

Graphic Design and Typography
Betty Binns

Printing
Studley Press, Dalton,
Massachusetts

PHOTOGRAPHIC CREDITS

Lynton Gardiner: cover; pp. 19, 21, 24, 26, 33-34, 37 (top), 44, 49, 53, 55, 57-59, 61, 63, 65, 66, 67 (bottom), 68

Yutaca Yoshii: p. 27, 35-36, 45-47, 67 (top)

Other photographs
p. 14: Courtesy Brooklyn Museum, Brooklyn, New York; p. 20, 25, 32: Courtesy of the Cleveland Museum of Art, Cleveland, Ohio; p. 23: Courtesy of the Smithsonian Institution, National Museum of the American Indian, New York, New York; pp. 25, 32, 60: Courtesy of the Honolulu Academy of Arts, Honolulu, Hawaii; p. 31: Michael Radtke; p. 37: Courtesy of the Peabody Museum of Archaelogy and Ethnology, Harvard University, Cambridge, Massachusetts; p. 41: Courtesy of the Ohio Historical Society; pp. 43 (Neg./Trans. no. 4114), 52 (Neg./Trans. no. 4115): C. Chesek, Courtesy of the Department of Library Services, American Museum of Natural History, New York, New York.

*Title and chapter opening
page drawing*
Based on an original drawing by Ann Peters, Orca-like figure from central ground of a Paracas mantle in the Göteborg Ethnographic Museet, no. 35.32.187

Fernando Guellees & Caroleun
Carlos Cornejo f Serena
Fernando Rojas Lardumont
Juan y &   Bush Meadows.
Elizabeth Wroobel

General Salazar Monroy.